# Enemy secrets in the house of God for the advanced

# Enemy secrets in the house of God for the Advanced

## Prophetess McRae

XULON PRESS

Xulon Press
2301 Lucien Way #415
Maitland, FL 32751
407.339.4217
www.xulonpress.com

© 2022 by Prophetess McRae

All rights reserved solely by the author. The author guarantees all contents are original and do not infringe upon the legal rights of any other person or work. No part of this book may be reproduced in any form without the permission of the author.

Due to the changing nature of the Internet, if there are any web addresses, links, or URLs included in this manuscript, these may have been altered and may no longer be accessible. The views and opinions shared in this book belong solely to the author and do not necessarily reflect those of the publisher. The publisher therefore disclaims responsibility for the views or opinions expressed within the work.

Unless otherwise indicated, Scripture quotations taken from the King James Version (KJV)–*public domain.*

Paperback ISBN-13: 978-1-66286-382-0
Ebook ISBN-13: 978-1-66286-383-7

I will pour out My Spirit on My people to punish the enemy through the anointing that I will place upon My chosen ones. I am rejoicing in the great victory that is about to spring forth. I will fulfill all that I have called into being. I have come to destroy the works of the enemy, and I will work through My people to do just that. I am going to break the bronze gates and release the promises that I have given to My people. What I have promised will come forth in the power of My kingdom. It will come to rest even as a mantle upon the shoulders of My beloved. I will bring you into your birthright and bring forth destiny. You will walk knowing that you carry My authority, says the Lord... thus say's the Lord by... The Spirit Of Prophecy Bill & Marsha Burns.

The line between the Anointing and WITCHCRAFT are So close and thin YOU had better Know God to be able to tell the difference in My Sistergirl Voice there are a many of good people who are believers that practice witchcraft .

Good and Evil is on the same tree. In the same garden (eve)

Some Pastors are real with God, serving with all they've got" and their spouse is practicing Witchcraft laying snares around the Church, and doing evil against it's members.. controlling the church through their position, and those that are living with such, God bless them they have not the slightest clue, Good and evil live on the same tree in the garden.. and on the same street in many neighborhoods, We do good to know the difference, Just because it's a move in the spirit We automatically think its God.. and its Ok but we are not to remain unaware "Know the difference!!! .. Witch Craft is a system and not an event or happenstance chance Its a system of bewitchment, "Its a set up trap of evil operations their aim Is to deceive our senses and frustrate our plans

Everyone wants to be bigtime and have a well Known name, with lots of members, Many Trees with a lot's of leaves.. But No Fruit. Is how I feel about churches Today Many are or IS becoming social clubs With Motivational Speakers Here In Oklahoma There One that has a social gathering In the sanctuary They serve wine so I'm told I don't mean to be judgmental but where I'm from the sanctuary is supposed To be a holy place this should not be.

I know there are Many Who Agree.

People shooting up the church.. God Talks! he reveals the secrets of the enemy and those who are at work for him.. If you spending any kind of time with him, if you paying attention to your dreams .. Some of you need to take a day off work and get in his face see what the kids are doing, see what going around you.. God Talks" I'm Re minded

when my children were small, i would laugh at them at times they'd be done something while I was away, when I'd return they run to me trying to explain themselves.. But first they'd ask.. "Did God tell you anything?"

I walk in some churches and some of the people act as if I'm like the church police

The Witches to be exact and those that have something to hide. I had one pastor tell me .. how I betta not tell her secret.. how she had placed voodoo under the church steps so that her members wouldn't leave her church.. Jesus Talks, I No longer call you servant because a servant doesn't know his masters buss but I call you friend. that's scripture.. they wanted Me out their buddy" at any cost

It got so bad one time "I couldn't even put my address on the offering envelops.. I came up through the church Hard there be times I'd get in the closet in my bedroom for hours I wasn't married at that time.. and i be crying so hard that My stomach would be shaking, laying on the floor.. My children knocking at my door "Mama you ok"? Id hear there lil voices fussing with each other.. she praying" shut up My Son.. "Well ask her can we have some Cereal'.? eyes swollen I'd go to the church no one would sit near me, Or should I say was allowed too, If the first lady didn't care for you.. no one else was allowed too either. I kid you not, once I was sitting on one side of the church by myself the whole church on the other side.. But God wouldn't allow Me to leave.. I did leave once and he sent me right back.. "DAG gone it!.. I had to go back " I felt like I was in a lifetime movie," all alone on the plant, I can laugh now" but back then. Jesus Jesus Jesus.. but any way, the Wc Objects things I was moving from around the Church "You'd never guess who was putting it there after all.. Trying to keep people she did-int want to come to the church.. at bay.. Oh I could go on.

But my point is..

God was getting Me ready for today... either you gonna love Me' or Hate Me.. But I'm coming.. God has been hiding me for a long time, at times couldn't make an innocent trip to the grocery store sometimes.. But I didn't go through all that for nothing".. I tried to come out and do Ministry,conference calls lines, Blog talk radio recordings, all before time

Had a dream last night that all My enemies were in one Car together, and the CAR caught FIRE and I was standing on the outside of the Car, and I could see them burning inside the Car.. Male& Female screaming at me" and calling Me Names.. I even saw some children in the car.. OMG "But yes I did..

I was going through something once, and I ask God who was behind it? and he told Me small hands.. So I understood why I saw the children in the burning car. "I recorded in my first book how people use children to get into places where they can't witches teaching the children what to do"

I had no one to tell me what was going on with me.. I knew not of any book to read ..why was God showing me all this" at that time" I thought, crazy stuff.. dreams were clear he wake me up and tell me go to the church NOW 2'am 3 am .not knowing for what" id get the instructions when id get there .. he'd have me to move something things around the church Yes "witchcraft stuff .. he'd show me what to remove it's like he would point it out to me and Id zoom in on it.. There were times I though I was Nuts not Crazy but Nuts…(mid 90's) just me and the holy spirit.. I'd tried to talk to my leaders my old Pastor, Pastor Quick all he'd say is" Sister Tammy God is going to use you mightily and he'd hold the sister Tammy part like a song.. I loved and highly respected him and still do and always will

. He told Me… "The thing that is holding You Sister Tammy you're gonna be holding it; I call it the trash bag box story.. each time I get to the last trash bag in the box that was holding the trash bags when I get to the last bag The box that was holding the bags go's into that last bag.. now that thing that was holding me I'm now I'm' holding it..

I want you never to forget What I told you about CHILDERN 1 Samuel 20:40 this wicked people use children to lay snares and all sorts of

Evil, they teach it to them, Now here Jonathan uses the lad to retrieve the arrows while he sent a secret message to David, David was hiding from Saul at the time This Story was Not evil at all but just an example, My Point is beware of Some Children Today. And Witches are Big on placing their snares under trees's

There are demonic forces that are at work against us they aim to keep us from reaching our goals. Jesus Want's to see his people set free from poverty, sickness Sin and shame, bondage oppression he hears the Cries of his people and is very attentive to Our Cry he hears Our silent cry.

Hebrews 4:15 For We do not have a high priest who is unable to sympathize with our weaknesses.

He feels our pain the enemy desires to keep us oppressed and confused Jesus wants us to know that we have the victory over the Devil Everyday all day not just sometime, but all the time. Scripture declares that he will never leave us or forsake us and he wont My heartbeat is to educate the body of Christ on the Many deceptive strategies of Satan on all levels; he has a three fold agenda to... Steal, Kill, and Destroy" but how?" he fights us on this type of teaching more than anything because he knows if you ever wake up" you'll never go back to sleep again; We have to deal with the spiritual realm so that we'll be affective in the natural realm because we've put things in place in the spiritual first. Just getting stirred through sermons stimulating our minds and emotions and people are leaving out the same way they came in.. Is no good"

I like this scripture..They have healed also the hurt *of the daughter* of my people slightly, saying, Peace, peace; when *there is* no peace. Jeremiah 6:14 KjV and for this reason I believe many will become offended and fall away, because things didin't work out the way they wanted them to, because of hard times and all the spiritual battles; they've harden their hearts against the creator and have falling away, AS the kingdom of God advances so dose the attacks against it we are in an advancing war, the enemy is attacking from the inside and the outside, on yesterday I was feeling out of pocket I guess you could say" off like, just wrong" Id slip off and pray for a minunite "Lord what's wrong I'd humbly ask, Well My attention was drawn to this large box full of old warfare notes that I've collected over the years" something that needs to be cleaned out and organized; "to be honest,.. "I saw the edge of this one little piece of paper sticking out" yelling at me! Pull me out"

so I did and it read... The enemy wants you to be in bitterness of soul, so that you won't focus, and to act out when there is no real fear or danger!

This really blessed me, and my peace returned, but my point is.. The enemy wants us to lose our creditability, our testimony, our focus, and act out" and look crazy; when there is nothing to fear and no real danger, Wow thank you Father" this was for sure one of Satan's tactics to play on my emotions.. " When I heard the voice of the Lord tell me to write this book' I'm like Lord you can choose anyone you sure you want me to do it"? I guess you can say I saw myself as a grasshopper, I'm not the office administrative type; and I could hear one of my old longtime buddies sarcastically saying to me..." and you think" Jesus didin't know that?" that your not the administrative type?

I've been Studying Spiritual Warfare for twelve years or so", along the lines of the Occult and Demonic Forces ,Astral Projecting Witches; and the Snares they lay around People's Homes Car's and Job's sometimes I'll just move the Snare and the Person will never know" that something evil was set up for them," then other times God will have

Me to make the person aware... As My Old Brother n Law would say" ("School Em Sis") and raise them up"..Ministering to those suffering from demonic affliction and Occultic Powers and "I must say I love my Job' I'm not afraid of Witches, Demons, or those who do Voodoo, Hoodoo Black Magic, Root Workers and nether should you be, there is more with us then with them 2 kings 16:16 ...I've had multiple death curses sent out against me, and graveyard dirt placed in my yard .God and nobody but God saved me from everyone of them attacks. I know who holds the Power, They didin't give Me My life and they can't take it away... It's like coming to a Gun fight with a Knife or a yard stick before one could raise their arm to swing.." well it would be all over in a matters of seconds. One must know who they are In Christ Jesus and the authorhy that he has given and most importantly who he is; The Almighty All Knowing, All Seeing ,Powerful God, rest in him the Holy Spirit will lead and guide Us through every situation often times when we're in heating circumstances going through life's storms or those seasons of testing, seasons of crazy, we all have them ,when your trying to explain and the more you try to explain, the more crazy and off balance you sound.. your Grandmother" would look at you and say" that's alright baby" and people will tell you "just trust God" (those times) The scripture tells us after we've done all that we can do just stand and along with that standing taking on the position of quietness wouldn't hurt when we give something to God, that means it's not up for discussion, "you know" there are some who mean well " when they ask about your previous situation, and like the sodomite woman" all is well If you choose to" let them know, that you have turn it over to the Lord and you keep step"n.. Spiritual Warfare is about Territory guarding your gates, keeping all that the father has intrusted to you, Satan will only yield at the ground that has been taken from him, that doesn't mean he won't try to get in, I remember one night in my home I was praying closing the gates in the spirit realm and I locked them in Jesus name.. around my home, family, life my mind my sleep etc: Well shortly thereafter I'm done praying, and getting ready for bed and the holy spirit speaks to me.." the enemy is trying to jimmy the lock" and sometimes along with a message of alert such as this one a face will flash before me someone I recognize and other times not recognize but nevertheless God is so faithful; There is a a book by John Ramirez.. Out Of The Devil's Cauldron: John give his life's testimony about how God saved and delivered him from Satanism, and in the book he tells how at night he would fly around to neighborhoods and pronounce spells and curses on the people who lived there, but some neighborhoods he said all he could do was land ONLY land there he couldn't leave any spells because it was prayed over and dedicated unto the Lord; so he'd band on a few stop signs kick over some potted plants a flower or two but that's about all he could do.

The gates had been closed and locked and and the enemy had no choice but to yield;

HEDGE YOUR LIFE

As God's Minister you must hedge your life fence yourself ;if you are going to fulfill the calling God has for your life this is a very important fact, Remember in Job 1:10 the enemy couldn't even get close to Job his home or his property because of the fivefold hedge Of Protection.

Dr. D.K Olukoya Wrote that in ancient times, gates were very important because the safety of a city was determined by the strength of the gate. There are spiritual gates and physical gates, gates of fire, there are gates that lead to the city of a Persons life so; get into the habit of closing the gates around you. Your heart your head, your stomach, navel, your soul, we will look at the soul in more depth later on, But also your hair I was having my car repaired at the tire shop with new breaks pads, and while I was waiting I heard the holy spirit say .. close the gates around your car.. I can remember the repair man coming into the waiting area and he gave me a funny look, I close the gates around everything even My day" the work of my hands, this prayer anything I'm about to do, start or finish Father I close the gates of protection around this book and the person reading it and their families from all evil in Jesus Mighty Name.

As we arrive closer to the return of our Lord and savior The adversary and his demons are not taking a rest but are bent on destruction even the more to derail and deceive the body of Christ with all sorts of concoctions but after reading this simple little life changing book you will be well aware of them and walk in your governmental Authorhy.

MONEY: MONEY: MONEY:

For the love of money is the root of all evil, some people ,eager for money, have wondered from the faith and pierced themselves with many griefs 1Timothy 6:10 NIV

Money is so sweet , but there are a lot of things that accompany money deep things that the ordinary eye cannot see. Trading has many evil practices pay cash as often as you can. I read that Secret Societies Members don't give out cash but will buy for the person in need. they will never allow their money to be seen. Dime abuse, Penny abuse, I use to see a dime or penny laying around and think nothing of it such a small amount of money, but when God gave me wisdom sometimes these coins have been placed in a place for satanic and demonic purposes to bring bad luck if you will" the coin could be placed down on heads for good luck and tails for evil or bad luck I seen people make marks on the face of the coin concerning the area they wish to target for affliction the eyes, mouth, or head or Shoulders for instance .. let's say the person is like going to a meeting where they must talk using all their vocabulary Knowledge the evil person will assign a evil spirit to the face of that coin targeting the mouth and placing it somewhere near the person as close as they can and the evil energy will effect the outcome by interfearing with the delivery of the persons speech. let me share some of the scenarios I've seen centered around this.. In folklore magic Voodoo, Hoodoo I read that Money Is used In Spells to Draw in more Money Or To prevent Money from coming, I once knew of a young Man who didn't have any drivers licenses and he drove where ever he wanted but always with a penny on heads down beside him on the floor of the vehicel, he believed this would keep the authorities at bay, There was an unfaithful boyfriend who was seeing two young ladies at the same time, and when one was over visiting he would open the door and lay a coin in the front door threshold of his house heads down to keep the other woman away while he spend time with the other, and remove the coin when he was done, place another there heads up to pull the other to him this was done so that the two visiting ladies would never cross paths. There was a girlfriend I had name Colette A very attractive young lady, one day her jealous boyfriend dropped her off at my home" I greeted her at the door and asked "Colette where's your car?" She replied at the house, girl I ' haven't moved my car all week Byron's been driving me around she shifted from side to side, she was holding a child on her hip, after visiting with me for a while, I drove her back to her home approx a 10 min drive; when we arrived" there was her car backed into the driveway with a penny tucked under the driver side front tire face down, I pointed it out to her and told her to remove it. There was a woman who disliked her boss so she would lay coins at her office door. face down to try and bring bad luck to her day, Black Bobbie Pins, nails to hold her down keep her in place if she didin't want her to leave that way she could leave if someone needed to stay back it wouldn't be her ... .Witchcraft Manipulation And Control, these types of doings are from the Black Arts And Occult And should not be taking likely. I've learned that some people don't know what there really doing, the truth behind it, they see it as a trick that my grandmother, grandfather uncle willie taught me. DEMONIC MONEY

Money is another tool that the enemy use's to form a demonic hold on someone, evil people have been known to pray evil witchcraft prayers and burn demonic candles over Money $$$

and give the evil gift to the person they dislike; hardly no one is likely to turn down money.

When I receive money like that I pray over it binding and rebuking any curses attached to it covering it in the precious blood of Jesus Christ Yashua

also the same when I'm the giver ... Hevenly Father In the Name Of Jesus I pray and cover this let's say $ 20.00 Bill I'm giving in the blood of Jesus every penny every nickle and dime and quarter that makes up this 20 dollar bill, My good deed will not turn on Me and be used for evil against Me, or My finances In way shape, form, fashion or design. This also is a Prayer to be prayed after praying for someone else.. Backlash Retaliation

*When we stand in the gap for another there is a link in the spiritual realm *connecting the two parties like a power cord that electricity can flow back and forth through to the person praying , So You Immediately Cut and Sever all the links and ties leading back to you, and Father I wish not to partake of the leaven from the prayer I prayed for (Lisa) I close and lock all doors given access to Me.. Thank you Father In Jesus Name.. Amen And you can literally feel the link when it disconnects.

The soul begins in God's will, but the purpose of the evil spirit is to draw it off into the carrying out of his will the (evil spirit) by counterfeiting the guidance of God.. Jessie Penn Lewis-

The Enemy and his little demonic crew has been running race tracks around us for a long time but God is going to establish us and make our foundation sure, If we be moved it won't be by means of demonic control, Amen We will see him ahead of time no matter what or who he tries to hide behind or in, it will all be in Vain. "You Know I wish that there were no evil people in the world "but of course that would be showing a great lack of common sense; just as sure as Satan Is Satan and he walked to and from on the earth in the book of job, looking for someone to devour there is evil upon the earth. Just as we follow Jesus he also has followers as well, and the bible lets us know that he comes to steal kill and destroy and so does his followers (his agents) People that follow Satan has no future, because he doesn't have one; He hates God and the people of God, the Church.. he wants to infiltrate the Church he and his Satanic agents they want to acquire secret information revelations that we receive.. I often wondered how can someone who really doesn't have a heart for Jesus spend so much time in the church around the Children of God and God things? Its because their studying to deceive, Not to Obey and we the children of God must be wise as a Serpent and gentle as a dove. Jesus is getting us ready preparing us for this end time deception things ahead. The Anti Christ is both a person and a evil spirit' and is already in the world john 2:18 this is how we know that this is the last hour. It is about Man making himself his own god following his own will the man of lawlessness the man or woman doomed for destruction he will exalt himself over everything that is called God or is worshiped so he sets himself up in God's temple proclaiming himself to be God. 2 Thessalonians 2:3

I believe this is why it's so easy for his agents to come on in the house of the lord and take a seat and begin their beguiling seducing influence against the ones that have been set apart for a sacred service unto the lord.

The Enemy wants to bring us to shame by attacking us with everything possible for us to begin to doubt our salvation and faith, just one battle after another to the point that you don't know what to do, his goal is to take away the light from our eyes anything that makes you and I smile, by manipulating behind the scenes, and we need the revelation and insight to push in prayer and war effectively and hit the target, and shut the enemy down the kingdom of heaven sufferth violence and the violence take it by force- force in prayer loosing binding overthrowing casting down canceling rebuking using the keys of the kingdom. If you are holding kingdom key's you must have revelation knowledge about different types of spirits and what role they play against the body of Christ. I'm going to educate on occultic powers and demonic spirits. I believe that the closer we get to the return of Jesus Christ the son of the living God the Anti Christ is turning up the heat and pulling out all the stops bent on destruction to derail the body of Christ inventing new way's to conjure up new evils and we are not to be afraid but aware. I heard another Minister of the Gospel say we the Christians have the power to break this stuff and Cancel it's effect, but we're the ones running from it.. someone's chasing you with a stick, and your holding a loaded gun in your hand and your the one running".. Picture that" Fear God not people. To win souls sometimes we're going to have to get in peoples faces, not trying to be popular or show off our ability of how good we can talk, not trying to have the biggest Church. Satan's kingdom is growing and expanding because we're not doing enough using our authority ..witchcraft has a serious offense anyone that plays around with Witchcraft and or the occult has a curse of death upon them and the may even look like death in their appearance and in their eyes. I was surprise to learn that people go into the graveyards at night to preform evil ritutials I was on my way to work one evening and I heard the Holy Spirit Say to Me "Come Against Graveyard Curses. I didin't know of the demonic power of this Occult Ritual, people have been doing this for generations It is a double forbidden By God.. Isaiah 66:17

Isaiah 66:17 New International Version (NIV)

17 "Those who consecrate and purify themselves to go into the gardens, following one who is among those who eat the flesh of pigs, rats and other unclean things—they will meet their end together with the one they follow," declares the LORD.

These are they who seek salvation in the religions abominations of man they shall be consumed together, the scripture go's on to say.. I the Lord know your works and your thoughts, because God knows both their thoughts and their works he shall come in furious judgment upon them, God is displeased with this kind of carrying on..

Malachi 3:5 New International Version (NIV)

5 "So I will come to put you on trial. I will be quick to testify against sorcerers, adulterers and perjurers, against those who defraud laborers of their wages, who oppress the widows and the fatherless, and deprive the foreigners among you of justice, but do not fear me," says the LORD Almighty.

**I'd like to warn you of the graphic explicit nature of this ritual Necromancy**

**I'm going to tell you the inside information concerning this Grave ritual magic and also give you the prayer points so you can hit the target directly in prayer and shut this door It's time for plan speaking someone needs to inform the body of Christ what these Wacky Folk are doing now' some just believe that they can just lift the burden of human suffering when a problem arises in their on lives. and of course their are others that strongly wish to inflict harm and misfortune on others because of evil black greedy and jealous hearts**

so much of occult knowledge is at the worlds finger tips; and people are not only logging on to these sights every day" but are experimenting and becoming snared by them.

Remember that Jesus Christ is all power, more than the devil and the powers of darkness. Put on your spiritual Armour and be filled with his spirit and obey the Lord in all things.

They believe that the graveyard dirt is not as important as the person in the the grave for example to preform a Love spell they' who practice such a thing would go to the grave of a person who they knew loved them while still alive and that would be Incorporated into their spell workings, the dirt is an object that corresponds with the traits of the person buried beneath it. In Haiti French Anthropologist Alford Metraux Observed a Phenomenon Called

(Sending Of The Dead) This freak Me Out! Who in their correct mind Lord"?

**Voodoo Deaths and Hexes Curses:**

In this ritual the sorcerer or sorceress, witchdoctor, herbalist commands their client to go to a cemetery at midnight with offerings such as flowers, whiskey coins, silver dimes, methods by which one pay's for the graveyard dirt. It may vary from worker to worker but the principle is always the same. Their there to get in touch with an ancestral spirit and make a so called respectful application and payment. Beyond that there are numerous details for instance: whose grave, as I stated earlier (two) the kind of death they died and (three) where the grave is located, this is straight foolishness to me, I might add", but nevertheless I'm telling you it is very real' and strongly respected among theses witchdoctors and practitioners it has been practiced since bible times Necromancy is calling on the dead for information like Saul with the witch of doer, but this death by voodoo is another level in the occult black arts world, but once this secret of the enemy is out in the open, his kingdom has been dethroned of much evil power. At the end I will give you prayer points that will hit the target that will stop this evil work against you and your family and whatever else the father has given you to do.. (four) the location of the digging, the head for controlling the mind will emotions, the heart, for love, the feet for controlling one's going and coming. While researching for this book, reading the report of one witchdoctor he stated that he prefers the dirt of a solderers grave because they were strong and obedient. Sources say that no matter what's left weather dines pennies or whiskey it's how you place it down everything is done with a certain level of respect, People who do this crap, believe that if they pay for it' the dirt is more effective, because there is a huge difference between capturing a person which is unlawful.. enslavement) and offering to pay for the persons spirit services which they believe is an honest transaction of employment. Honest, "Somehow I kinda believe they need to rethink that thing" but nevertheless moving right along…

Graveyard dirt is a magical link,

they take dirt from the gates of the cemetery from a newborn baby, tot or a person that was murdered, what ever the ritual calls for that corresponds with what effect their trying to archive.

The third grave on the left, or the seventh grave, the silver spoon for dipping I read that " If wanting to harm more than one person a scoop of dirt is taking for each person.

There are quite a bit of levels to be uncovered on this particular topic, but I am determined to expose all I can, and then build a prayer point list for the main things to be cast down in Prayer." I hear in my spirit the Lord telling me to to tell you you not to be afraid" greater is he who is in us than he who is in the world. 1 John 4:4 We are from God and We have overcome them.. This is knowledge.. The Secrets Of The Enemy That he' doesn't want revealed

The area's that we are blind to is where Satan and his agents are gaining ground at, I always say this topic is not for discussions every waking morning but jut being able to recognize it when it is near by" just as one could identify a certain ingredient in a cooked dish. .

Isaiah 8:19 Say's " And when they say to you seek those who are mediums and wizards who whisper and mutter, should not a people inquire of their God? Should they seek the dead on behalf of the living?

What logic is there in seeking the dead on behalf of the living? This is a form of Necromancy communication with the dead, especially in order to predict the future this is sorcery , black magic, witchcraft, occultism which is sternly and strictly forbidden by God.. It is a serious and severe matter that will be judged harshly... Malachi 3:5King James Version (KJV)

5 And I will come near to you to judgment; and I will be a swift witness against the sorcerers, and against the adulterers, and against false swearers, and against those that oppress the hireling in his wages, the widow, and the fatherless, and that turn aside the stranger from his right, and fear not me, saith the LORD of hosts.

The bible clearly speaks against the cult of spiritsim which is one of the oldest pagan religions known to mankind, Jehovah God forbid such practices because there was and is no light in them. Verse 20 those that neglect this standard of truth they shall find no answer in their day of anguish, and shall be driven even further into the impenetrable darkness. A now delivered set free by the blessed power of God.." Satanic herbalist shared that the people that would come to see her for her services on healing, for instance maybe for pain in the Stomach area She wouldn't tell them that the pain will leave from their stomach and now go to their Leg, Why"? Because Only Jesus Christ Can totally heal a divine healing.

King James Bible...Isaiah 31:1 Woe to them that go down to Egypt for help; and stay on horses, and trust in chariots, because *they are* many; and in horsemen, because they are very strong; but they look not unto the Holy One of Israel, neither seek the LORD!

The Scripture warns that ...Your covenant with death will be canceled (annulled) and your pact (agreement) with Sheol will not stand when the overwhelming scourge sweeps by you will be beating down by it.. Isaiah 28:18

**PRAYER:**

In the name of Jesus Christ I rebuke all illegal covenants with death against My Life, My Marriage, My Ministry, My Goals, My Family, My Destiny No Weapon formed against My life shall prosper , I shall live and not die, In the name of Jesus any covenant with the death and the grave against my life shall not stand. Every cursed spoken or placed against my life either joking or seriously.. Blood of Jesus wash it away now, Any curse issued upon my life by former evil friends I rebuke cancel and overthrow it and replace it with well wishes in the mighty name of Jesus Christ. I ask you heavenly Father to breathe life back into Me, And I Silence all evil alters calling my name, every Satanic Coffin constructed for Me fall down and die, every spirit of death against my goals receive the fire of the holy ghost In Jesus Name.

Let every offer offered be denied In Jesus Name.

Things To Rebuke Bind and Cage:

- Company Graveyards
- Graveyard Walk Around
- Choice Graves.. On Left Or Right and So Forth
- Nine Pinnies
- Thirteen Pinnies
- Whiskey
- Nine Needles
- Candles Of All Colors
- Seventh Grave
- Silver Spoon
- Dirt Magic
- Location Of Their Dig..Head, Heart, Feet,
- Payment Offering
- Placement Of Payment
- Cemetery Gates
- Rebuke All Spirit Services, Those listed here and those that are unknown To Me
- Their Fetch Of Ancestral Spirits
- Always Rebuke Their Concentration
- All The Exchanges.. Garments, Shoes, Etc, (just whatever) It could be anything.

When these spirits are at work in someones life they will have dreams about death and seeing deceased family members in dreams. Their life will seem dead just existing not living, no life or light in their eyes in many situations people that are plagued by these spirits are often walking time bombs on the verge of exploding. I Pray That the healing power of God begin to flow to every part of your Body And Send Out Every Spirit Of Death In Jesus Name.

*I am* he that liveth, and was dead; and, behold, I am alive for evermore, Amen; and have the keys of hell and of death. Revelation 1:18

Christians walking in the knowledge and power of their God given spiritual authority are especially targeted for attention by the enemy, because their the ones that know who they are' and are the most threatening to the enemy's Kingdom and are able to bring the demonic assignments to a screeching dead end halt. The kingdom of darkness respects power when power and power meet face to face the lesser power has to bow. Power will recognize power even if it's not as strong as the power it' passes by, with out touching or making contact an energy surge current is released.. They know who we are The True Saints Of God, The carriers of the fire. A warrior is a person that specializes in combat or warfare.

One thing that brings a holy fire out of me is what I call Religious Deception In the church.

4Jesus answered, "See to it that no one deceives you. 5For many will come in My name, claiming, 'I am the Christ,' and will deceive many. 6You will hear of wars and rumors of wars, but see to it that you are not alarmed. These things must happen, but the end is still to come....Matthew 24:5

Imposters in the church..

Just a moment ago my middle daughter telephone me to inform me that one of her co-workers lost his only Son, Gun down in a hotel room dressed as a woman waring a wig & lipstick. It's believed that he deceived a man into believing that he was a woman, and when time came to show and prove he could not" this is beyond terrible news for any parent to have to hear my heart go's out.

But this is a form of deception the person was deceived thinking this man was a woman when he was not" I don't find this amusing in any way, but deception abounds.. and we must be aware and on guard..

**Matthew 7:15-20King James Version (KJV)**

15 Beware of false prophets, which come to you in sheep's clothing, but inwardly they are ravening wolves.

Inwardly," What are we Inwardly? Whatever is in our heart is what is what the devil will use, this is why we must cast down those vain imaginations so the enemy won't have anything to hook onto, I do' what I call heart checks, asking the if there is anything in my heart that shouldn't be there, because things could be there and we are unaware time has buried it; I was reading a book once and in the middle of the page it suggested the reader stop and and ask the lord to show you if you have any unforgiveness in your heart; I searched my mind tossed around a few thoughts I revisited" came to the conclusion I'm good, well after praying the prayer the Holy Spirit reminded me when I was 21 my aunt would come down from N.Y.C and would bring gifts for my other girl cousins every time she would come home from the city, she would bring gifts shoes, clothes Etc and would distribute them right in front of me; and I'd watch them as they would admire their gifts we living in the south at that time" and nothing around there could ever compare to the likes of anything coming from the big city of N.Y and each time she'd get to the end of her bag of gifts; there was never anything for Tammy" but I'd never let her know that this bothered me, I'd play it off as if I didin't care, I'd even tell my cousins how nice I thought their gifts were; I'd never asked my aunt why didn't she bring me anything; but I" could see in my cousins eyes they wanted to ask her, but they kept quiet; Well this being so many years ago over 25 years it was dead and berried and long forgotten.. but it was in there UNFORGIVENESS and bless the Lord he reminded me of it. So things could very well be hidden within our hearts.. Heart Check, Heart Check.

Now everybody who knows Me knows that I always come against witchcraft and witches in our churches, God has given me the ability to discern a witch and there has been times he has hid it from me for a season I think at times he had to hide it from Me at times was due to my immaturity there is a way that God wants us to handle what he has reviled to us and now I've learn that after he allows me to see the truth Watch" again I say "Watch for a while, but to be honest I would like to stand up no matter where I am and yell to the very top of my lungs .. WITCH WITCH WITCH !!! Because most of the time they are undercover in the marketplace in the community and of course in the Churches and we need to discern watch for a while see what their up too" who are they targeting? "now I'm' sure it would be leadership their ultimate goal is to topple the Church the Pastor his Marriage and reputation they are working for Satan under a Lie that he is going to bless them in some type way and they they would receive more evil power you know' move on up the evil latter, Prophetic Ministries are always targeted A Ministry that is sound in faith and the Word of God are strongly targeted, they want the Church to loose it's Strength and Structure they want to find out where the or who is the strongest link, the structure of the Church or Business Marriage, Friendship etc: or what ever they have in their design like pulling that main thread and everything starts to unravel. And they want to remove anyone they feel that may be a potential threat to them and are aware of who they are.. Now" this is where it gets deep... I've been through this a hundred times, when they know that your on to them, they will do anything to protect their identity and their well respected prominent

Name even Kill. They already know who they want to eliminate upon their arrival, that would be a resistance to what their trying to do. This demonic operation is well organized, They even have sleepers waiting to be called and placed, Placed in our School Systems, Government offices, Churches, Youth Groups, Military, Police. So they send in on assignment to remove and take out certain ones in leadership Position and replace them with their evil Man or Woman. They Infiltrate. I started going through these crazy things before I even knew who I was in the kingdom Of God<<< Laying snares for my feet ...Psalms 140:5 and also Job 30:12 laying down demonic and satanic objects for me to walk over putting these type things in my path the way they knew that I had to go in order to get to my assigned place Psalms 142.. I'd find things near my Car, either tucked down by the tires, or in front of My Car door, that wasn't there when "I got out of My Car when I arrived, I've learned to pay attention when getting in and out of My Car now a days' the work place is crucial for this type of carrying on ....For among my people are found wicked men ,they lie and wait as one who set's snare. They set a trap to catch men as a cage is full of birds, so their houses is full of deceit .Jeremiah 5:26-27 ..But there is so much information here that I want to share concerning how they strategize and plot and lay snares It's not only going to be things that one could see with the natural eye it's also much done in the spiritual realm as well, Their Job also is to find out the telephone numbers and address of their targets, who their friends are, who their children are and who their friends are, looking for an open door, someone that has close access to your home and to you. They will give demonized gifts, and I've found that things with scripture on it or bible base books, clothes something worn on the body Money etc will be used the most as a gifts. Demonic Hugs and Kisses, rubbing themselves with oils and lotions before love making, hand shaking, Etc fingernail clippings, your hair, personal things that come directly from your body dispose of yourself, Menstruation Pads don't leave in the restroom of anybody's home, or Work Place neatly wrap it up and expose of someplace else.

I read a Woman's Story about how her own Sister had taken her used Menstrual pad from the bathroom trash and taken it to a voodoo occult worker, and placed a curse on her, by way of that item, that beheld her DNA the curse was that she would never have babies.. she was extremely jealous of the older Sister, this evil thing was done at 23 years of age, at a time when the older Sister came home from college, years later the Sister Married, and 5 years had come and gone; no children after much Prayer, Depression, Tears, Many Doctor visits, Loss of Money on expensive Medical Testing. One Lucky Day the younger Sister finally confessed what she had done, If I remember correctly the evil worker had told the young girl to place the menstrual pad inside the Wall of an old abandoned house"

She was able to retrieve the Menstrual Pad after all those years and break the curse off her womb ...Sanctify the people, and say, Sanctify yourselves against to morrow: for thus saith the LORD God of Israel, *There is* an accursed thing in the midst of thee, O Israel: thou canst not stand before thine enemies, until ye take away the accursed thing from among you.. Joshua7:13

just need to be sure to ask Christ to please dress us every day in our spiritual Armour ..this is not to impart fear please don't be afraid.

Its just information; God has ordered your steps, and you belong to him. Now You may be saying to yourself this is crazy" who has the time and energy for this,"? They DO! If you are in the way of their Big satanic agenda to takeover and control Political and Economic Power, controlling Numbers, This is today's Sad reality. God so much so wanted this book written that he took me off the Job" Jesus loves us and he strongly wants us to be well informed , We have to be aware I heard one Man refer to it' as a satanic Pentecost so to speak" their looking forward to coming one day. Once they get all their people in place, some have even birthed children for certain agendas in these occults organizations ."now I feel lead to say' this is their corrupt mind set" and My assignment is to educate and expose It as best as I can, I'm no experienced Writer but I heard the Father say to Me" while sitting up in Bed One evening" Write A Book... So as if God the Creator of all things; is going to let them do all they wish to evilly do" without any interference from God They have really gone Mad.. God knew this kind of thing would rise up; Before the Foundation of the World Began .. BEFORE!!! (People) God has his People in place, he has holy Messengers that do his bidding psalms 103:20 around the clock all day, every day, and his gates and barriers that will block and stop and prevent them access .>>>the bible tells us that while men slept his enemy came and sowed tares" weeds) among the wheat and went away... Matthew 13:25 They do this by doing witchcraft in the night hours, burning things, calling the persons name a certain amount of times your name is your soul, and they will attach their evil will to ones soul to make one feel heavy and sad weighted down not to mention the Mental confusion, Ezekiel 13: 17-18 ... When there's no visible reason to support these false feelings they ensnare Men's Souls Wanting to ware you down and remove you from your blessed place by having one feeling that they don't belong here or there >>>>They Can be the most prominent and well respected citizens in their towns and communities they are in Law Enforcement, Schools, Government Military Hospitals and you'd never know that they are, Who they are.

Their excellent at their profession weather it be a Nurse Or A, C.N.A Or A Waiter Of tables at A fine dining Establishment; highly trained to deceive they are, It baffled My Mind to know that There are Hospital Workers Doctors and Nurses that are involved in the Occult, these Doctors and Nurses are involved with human Sacrificing and Abortion. This is an easy way for occult workers to get blood" for drinking and other evil practices. The Brotherhood" and they used code names they don't call each other by their real names most of them are regular Church goers too so that they can fit in with Society, (noted) their

Church attendance will not be at a Strong Ministry or one that operates in the gifts of the Lord.. 1 Corinthians Chapter 12 ... When their on an assignment to to topple a Church or Corporation dept Head , I was informed by one now delivered Satanist that before entering A Religious Establishment She would be sure to leave My demons outside the building not to ever take them inside, She Said" I'd hang them on a tree because the demons had the ability to make you do something wired" perhaps in the middle of the service or something' and also she added" The person that prays over the service, if they are strong in the Lord, and not a luke warm christian the very minute they bind the powers of darkness in and over the service I would loose all my evil powers, So when praying over a Religious Service bind the powers on the outside as well as in the inside she ended. >>>

Now I had one Woman say (Quote) "I don't use my powers and knowledge on others unless their bothering me or I need to get myself or my love ones out of trouble she stated" well this is wrong too, any use of the Occult Wicca Divination or a Necromancer , The Practice of Magic arts of any kind at any time is Not OK in the Eyes Of God... Not Ever!

**King James Version And I will come near to you to judgment; and I will be a swift witness against the sorcerers, and against the adulterers, and against false swearers, and against those that oppress the hireling in his wages, the widow, and the fatherless, and that turn aside the stranger from his right, and fear not me, saith the LORD of hosts. Malachi 3:5**

**The Brotherhood, Satanic Worshipers are a secret cult I mentioned earlier they can be the most prominent renowned influential People that one could ever meet, But they hold a Evil Secret that they will protect with their life.**

Thank God for Rebecca Brown and the others the Hevenly Father allowed to come out and be free to tell the story.

They go through lengths to keep their meetings hidden, Its announcement of the meeting place is kept quiet until 2 hours prior and the Police is on guard to keep watch over the radio frequency while the meetings and ceremonies are being held everything is carefully planned, all bases are covered, there is even a Evil Satanic Throne transported to the meeting place..

The Evil Throne is Transported In a plain colored VAN... "I want to add right here I kept feeling a push from the Lord to hurry and add this.

These meetings and ceremonies are mostly held at full moons or to discipline someone. ( Alright I'll just keep My thoughts to Myself) "OK moving forward.. these meetings referred to as Black Mass Or Black Sabbath are hidden as far out and secluded as can be, Someone is in charge of set up and also the clean up after-wards, because of the sacrifices–ritual murders of animals and humans local mortuaries and crematories hospitals and even animal shelters are used to dispose of the bodies,all this is hush hush highly confidential and the parties involved are able to create control on the outside because they have people from all governments the higher up's it's an growing evil empire; It makes me think back 10 years or so, When things began to change such as Corporations and Government did some kind of switch from good is now evil and evil was now the new good, Satan's has his People in offices all across the World and their doing his bidding, but we've got to rise up the body of Christ and put things back in order teach our children the neighborhood children the ways of Jesus Christ support them with that new pair of shoes to keep them in school with confidence pushing them on through they are our future.

I've found that these demonic practitioners come into the Church and the first thing they'll do is get faked saved followed by fake tears and then be the best giver in the house until they feel this church depends on them, then they'll start to wanna call shots and test their power and influence. Their all for the Prayer Meetings if there's not one they'll promote one they make a big deal about prayer... feeling this would be something close to the Pastors heart, Satan's agent's know how to speak in tongues, Satanic Tongues, or demonic tongues which ever you prefer. When they do so they are sending out curses right there in the Church, or where ever their doing over the telephone on conferences calls prayer lines now they love the conference calls lines! these people have much influence a Strong influence, their good talkers, excellent in communication skills, they have so Many People fooled -bewitched -Maybe bewitched is a better Word; Don't Misunderstand Me"I'm not at all down Playing Prayer, these are the attributes of Satanic agents. Always pushing for smaller groups, Making valid points, they want to rid the Church of it's Older Stronger Members and Sants I call them the more seasoned ones. They'll be the loudest against any teaching against the adversary when the bible clearly tell us not to be ignorant of Satan's devices lest he gain advantage of us. 2 Corinthians 2:11... Day after Day

**1 Peter 5:8-9King James Version (KJV)**

8 Be sober, be vigilant; because your adversary the devil, as a roaring lion, walketh about, seeking whom he may devour:

**Satan Masquerades himself as an angel of light 2Corithians 11:14**

He is cleaver at disguises, a master deceiver. He Camouflages everything, the Holy Spirit will sound off an alarm letting us know that something here is off' not quite right" not lining up with the way of God; we may not be able to put an precise finger on it at the moment but the holy spirit is with us he is our helper ..So if stumble into a situation and your antenna start to send you warning signs don't ignore them, begin to cover yourselves in the blood of Jesus and close the gates of protection with fire against evil, around yourselves. Speak this with your Mouth "I in circle Myself about with Christ's divine Protection which no error May Set Foot.

ASTRAL PROJECTION... OR ASTRAL TRAVEL. OBE

Is becoming More and More popular among our young people, and they are teaching the ones under them so that it continues; even as I sit here and type and as you read on, just as someone is being born, someone is being thought.

someone could possibly be in your space and you're not even aware that they're there, basically your being Monitored, watched, observed, spied, upon, kept under surveillance, systematic review, and they do this by,A supposed form of telepathy that assumes the existence of a soul or consciousness called an astral body, that is separate from the physical body, The conscious mind leaves the physical body and moves into the astral body to experience what is called astral projection or astral travel.. aka OBE, The silver cord is the important part that keeps them astrally attached to their physical bodies, the silver cord is a valuable part of their connection..

Ecclesiastes 12:6

If ever the silver cord be loosed, or the golden bowl be broken, or the pitcher be broken at the fountain, or the wheel broken at the cistern.

**King James Version**

**Attachments, Power Cords.**

Lets take a quick look at these attachments..

Energy body attachments, In demonic possession cases studies it has been noted by demonologist that skin blemishes, growths, lumps, granulomas,and moles on the body can be due to energy body attachments or a witches mark but in this case attachments, as if one would hook a key chain to a belt loop.. if one would try to hook a keychain directly to his flesh every night it would most definitely leave a mark showing an attachment point. This attachment is a ground wire connecting the person to earth as they do their night errands; cut this attachment cut it with the sword of fire in Jesus name.

Sniffers.

As far fetched as it sounds, I assure you It is not, I thought that too, that I had heard It all, When I learned about the sniffers! Yes sniffers they can get a wift of a person's natural body odor and save it, until they want to locate that person in the spiritual realm, this can also be done by the perfume or cologne that a person wares, they hold your sent, and they are called sniffers, they can try to capture ones smell through a simple hug or just sitting near by.

Astral Projections.

This energy body has multiple layers and multiples energy centers called chakras, and these are something like vital body organs.. I have dealt with this type of wickedness for longer than I care to remember; Before I knew anything about OBE at times "I would feel as if there were another presence in the room Or I'd see a shadow pass by.. " you know those type of things you dare not mention, seeing things not there your officially ready for the funny farm. But I'm going to inform you on how to pray against this evil work,

Amen.. So from what I'm understanding This act is mostly done at night altho in my option it can be practiced anytime at will. Choosing a time at which he is sure that his target is asleep, they began by concentrating upon the person and imagines himself standing beside his target and then visualizes the cord which is called the Ray of Rapport (Power Cord) this cord looked at like a parent and child connection umbilical cord attached at both ends the Mother and the unborn fetus. . (cut this cord with the fire of the holy ghost at both ends severing it to be no more)...stretching from his friend out into space. After studying themselves as in calming themselves they are ready to take the leap onto the astral planes, with three intents of harm in mind called the forced deal.. that he or she want's to plant on his victim Malice, Lust, Vampire.

The Astral plans also called the Astral world is said to be plans of angelic existence intermediate between earth and heaven It's really the land of death states one practitioner; A place you know in your heart that one should not be.

It is said that these planes can be looked at like a light bulb that has three layers to it the inner layer, the middle layer, and of course the outter layer,

The Physical plane, The Astral Plane, The Causal plane... Glory be to God Send Fire upon everyone of them, Rebuke their travailing routes.

Curse, rebuke overthrow, with fire all these things, they are associated with this practice; This is one study that literately went on and on, the more information I found on this subject the more it kept coming It was just never ending; But I got the main points to overthrow in prayer and study subjects one can research for themselves.

- **Astral body Copy**

- Astral Energy
- Astral Animals Watchers and consciousness
- Energy Centers
- The energy body and all it multiple layers
- Astral Plans
- Astral Rounds
- Energy Storage Centers
- Exchange Pores
- Ida and Pingala winding up either side of the central channel
- Their Take Off
- The Hearing Of The White Noise
- The drawing of the energy from their chakara and feet
- The rotating of their hands
- Magnetic links
- Ray of light telepathic vision
- The ray direct connection
- All power cords
- Pentagrams, Hexagrams
- Psychic Substance
- Command vibrations unsteady
- Force deal type
- Shinning Cords
- Cut the Silver Cord from their Solar Plexus
- All Connections wires to space
- Tools, swords, Torches
- Obtain no records of Me
- Their Concentrating!
- Bring Down their Sympathetic system
- Central Channel called the sushumna running up through the center
- Bring down horse and rider
- Rebuke the demon holding up the physical body.
- The black line of substance, searing it off at the root

- Command them to be a wanderer in the lower levels with negative entities
- Rebuke their astral will
- Close off their energy loop, Cut off their energy flow and draw from the earth
- Rebuke their return back to the physical realm
- Confuse their aura checks, let it be filled with dirty spots
- Auric threads become extra thin, cut with fire
- Let Psychic lice overtake them.

The etheric body belongs to the sphere of the occult, it is not to be seen with the natural physical eye, although the anointed spiritual eye can, mostly prophets and seers can see in the spiritual realm what others cannot see. My goal is to inform the body of Christ that, we may" become more knowledgeable of Satan's devices, and not be taken captive by any means..

It reads in the books that the more wisdom that the astral body contains the more luminous it will be.. We're going to rebuke their astral light and their wisdom and Revelation. We know that the devil masquerades himself as an angel of light. IN the name of Jesus.. I will be sure to add prayer points at the end and as I go along. Some refer to them as watchers.. Watchers can also be instructed to follow or even eavesdrop on someone astrally or physically and then report back to their summoner.. The summoner can also summon a spirit to project for them, also note that a remote detection can be used and is said to be much stronger than just a normal watcher, (F-6 spirits) their called they're said to be like geniuses, these ones are called upon for use, when the summoner fears putting himself in harms way; they send out an evil worker to do his or her dirty work for them an astral animal , their secretly spying . It is Said that the summoning of the F-6 is suppose to cause more drain damage than projecting one self... So In the Mighty Name Of Jesus I command drain damage upon any

Astral Projecting Witch In Flight to My Home or anywhere I am.. In Jesus name. They use leylines and portals to travel through to place to place; shut their portals with fire and while their outside their bodies in a nubilous cloud it is a demon on the other end holding up their body while their out of it, they usually have someone watching over their lifeless corpse so no harm will come to it and the night travler will safely return from the astral plans.

From My experience I would know when they would arrive in my space I'd I'd hear a popping sound coming from high up in the corner of the room its always's the corner too they've made their entrance and also the same popping sound is heard when they've made their exit; often I'd would start to repeat Holy ghost fire over and over again, you could have handy a small water bottle it could be a small air freasher bottle like the

Kind you get for your car at the auto store fill it with water you could be sitting in your family room watching television and out of nowhere you hear a popping sound coming from the corner as I said the more advanced the lighter they'll be upon entering, Take that spray bottle of water spray it into the air in their direction they are not in their phycial body so they cannot withstand water or go through any of the elements but im sure that water is definitely a repellant for them, keep in mind that are like satan they do not want to be identifed once you know exactly who it is floating through your house / space the fun is over for them theyed rather remain anonymous another thing do not be afraid a fearless attitude is priceless once the school bully knows that your afraid of them oh', for sure your lunch money is theirs everyday for sure so walk with a fearless courageous attitude, also these nosey creeps can't move fast so' I hear that if you get up and leave the room they have trouble moving from point a to point b at a fast pace they have a slow float and if you pay close attention to the atmosphere you can feel the shift in the room and often times see a silhouette energy body floating around when they have entered in , something in a hazy foggy form, picture the smoke from a lit cigarette; the More advanced they are the more silent their entrance and exit will be, but pay attention to the atmosphere one meaning you" can sense another presence has entered if you pay attention to what your feeling the air in the room becomes thick and heavy, the astral body is fueled by energy fields cords of lights.. when I think about it Lucifer Bearer Of Light. It's a false light just like the astral traveler in their false light if I were to throw a glass of water in the air its too bad for them.

The pentagram matters much with the astral traveler.. well first lets look at this thing called the pentagram" I heard of it sure but didn't know the dynamics of it all I knew it was a tool used in witchcraft for evil, I knew that much" so one day this lady a seer, is praying over the telephone with me and one other lady and she tells me that she sees a pentagram and inside of it is my picture, in the middle of it;" I'm like what! Well not long ago the publisher of my first book (Warfare Strategies) whom I was very fond of and you can add (very" a few more times only to find out that this woman couldn't stand me did not like me at all" my husband told me that he wasan't feeling her but I sure was, she was smart and very anointed I was sending her offerings and supporting her ministry... So one day she calls and says hay daughter I need a nice picture of you for your book, well of course I sent to her, I'll make sure you get it back " its only for the book" me' Oh No problem sure I'll mail it today" a month go's by I had not receive the photograph back so I called her, and she informs me that her daughter was cleaning up for her and she accidentally threw it away and I am so sorry" she said.

So

#Come against their astral body separation, separation from their physical block# All three Astral plans Physical, Mental , and Astral, # Block all Portals and Ley Lines, Gateways Windows and Doors With Fire! the Refiners Fire, they have energy body attachments this is very important in their world cut it with fire

Overthrow the point of their Covenant meeting places this is where they refresh their spirit.# Cast down their etheric double framework. # It could be Projected as a long Rod or I think Maybe' a cord projected as a nebulous cloud connecting with the medium by a tenuous thread.

#Rebuke their take off# their spring board# Their Psychological Devices#

# their forms and symbols#

**The Occult And Water**

One day I was alone in my home I'll never forget walking from the bedroom into the living room area, and I heard the holy spirit say (Water Witch)

this made me go into an intensive study on this topic... Wow!!!

God's word tells us that we are destroyed for lack of knowledge!!This Kingdom must be studied fully. It is one of Satan's lest detected kingdoms; and most powerful demons reside and has most of the World under it's Full influence. This kingdom

works strongly and very close with the Fashion World, Entertainment Industry, and Make up; this is a deep revelation here, about the cosmetics that unfolded while researching and writing this book.. Now the evil one "Satan we know that he hates a woman because of Eve,

She bore our savior Jesus Christ.. God told him "Satan the Serpent" because you have done this thou are cursed above all cattle and above every beast of the field upon thou belly shall thou go and dust shall thou eat all the day's of thou life. And I will put enmity between thee and the woman, and between her seed and thy seed, and it shall bruise thy head ,and thou shall bruise thy heal. Genesis 3:14-15..

So upon this information Women will be his most targeted above all, now Men too, because they are the head and if the head is killed then the body dies along with it, But here we focus on the Woman... My Daughter informed me that getting your face done Up with Make Up is referred to as (Beat) getting your FACE BEAT.. these cosmetics have demonically been charged with demons that take away ones natural beauty in exchange for their own demonic beauty and within 4 months your skin will not look the same, holes and blotches to the point where one cannot go without it, and the more ones wares it the more ones gotta have it! Satan's goal is to have Women looking "BEAT FOR REAL!!! key word (BEAT)

It baffled me to find out, that make up, is demoniacally or can be demonically charged with witchcraft spells and demonic powers to seduce Men, for their Money, To make themselves irresistible to A Man, so to ware as he has no strength to withstand her or resist her...

Revelation 17:1-2 Say's And there came one of the seven angels which had the vials and talked with me, saying unto me come hither; I will show unto thee the judgment of the great Whore that sittith upon many waters: with whom the kings of the earth have committed fornication, and the inhabitants of the earth have committed fornication and the inhabitants of the earth have been made drunk with the wine of her fornication"

These demonic and evil Powers are also entwined into Clothen as well, to be sold in the stores; Half naked woman with the fake hair and nails showing lots of flesh has more than likely been in contact with the Marine Kingdom. You know the girls "I'm speaking of, the ones you see in the summer time and you make the comment .." it is not that Hot" Let me also say, I personally have Nothing against fake hair & Nails I'm a Woman too. ..through its Products Such as Make up, Cosmetics, Clothen, Jewelry, and Many perfumes fragrances Etc" these items are charged with demonic powers before being brought into the stores. It's so much here that centers around this Marine Kingdom,

Rev 12:12... I Want To Expose The The Class of Demons that Operate From Under The Waters, Oceans, Seas, Lakes, and Rivers, They Are Called Marine Spirits- The Water Kingdom

These Spirits Represent Witchcraft, Perversion, Lust ,Pride, Murder, Death ,Greed, Envy Rebellion, Destruction. You name it"

There are Many things that are Going on Under the Waters Which affects the lives of those on the Earth above. These Demons Can Conjure up Storms of Destruction and Cause Tragedy and Death and Loss of all kinds.

Unless Someone Discerns Their Manifestation And Rebukes them, Guess what? they can" and will take Over.

Matthew 8:26... When Jesus arose and rebuked the Wind and the Sea and the Bible says that there was a Grate Calm. he took Authority' over that Storm

if that storm had been a Natural Storm, Jesus Would Not have rebuked *something that was of his father.. He came to do the will of his Father.

He knew the storm was an Evil Manifestation of Water Spirits.

God is Exposing this Realm of Satan's Kingdom. It's Control Over Cites and the people.

We Must Pray That Gods Will be done Upon the Waters' the Voice of the Lord is Upon the Waters These Demonic Forces just want to reek Havoc in any and everything... They want You to give up on God and make one feel as if Whats the Use"? Depress and Oppressed You. Weigh you down with False burdens

God Is Mightier and Higher Then the floods and the Waves Gods kingdom Rules over all. Ps 89 The sea was Created to Praise God not to be Ruled by Demons. PS 98:7-8 God Will root out Rebellion from the Waters I want to make you aware of; please forgive me for jumping around I must admit I was being slow with completing this book, and the holy Spirit speaks to me and tell me," that I have 20 Twenty days to complete this book.. This Spirit carries a slavery Mentality to lust; Sexual Lust, and Alcoholism, Drugs, lying, (just an over do it!) and the list just go's on and on, the spirit of lust is never satisfied it keeps on going until it destroys it's victims, And I will list and enlightening you as much as I can, on all the the ends and outs, on these Spirit's characteristics," as the Lords Jesus Christ brings revelation, and It's My pleasure to do so... Amen. The spirit of Dog (Peppa) this spirit causes a Man to rape young children and family members and so forth.

Marine Kingdom Spiritual Deception

African Witchdoctors are Strong believers in Marine Witchcraft; Water Spirits they are Worshipers of them..Mami Wata

according to Ex Witchdoctors.

Many rituals are carried out with the use Of Water, running Water, flowing Water is believed to make a person leave town and go else where, Or causes restlessness or to walk at all times of the day and night even when it's unsafe to do so such as in a rainstorm or midnight. While researching this topic... Gathered Tracks or The Walking Foot Spell,

Wherewith thine enemies have reproached, O LORD; wherewith they have reproached the footsteps of thine anointed. Psalms 89:51..KJV

was one of many voodoo spells that is completed around large bodies Water, People's belongings are thrown into lakes and rivers, oceans for evil purposes; I was fabergasted to even learn that evil workers will use Holy Water from a baptism pool to perform a ritual! Rain water is often caught in jars, buckets, pales,and used to make Moon Water,

The Marine Kingdom is no doubt Satan's most prized possession there are many levels and avenues and degrees here that requires a Specialize Warfare

MARINE WARFARE... Just to name a few of the categories 's under the umbrella of The marine kingdom...The spirit husband and spirit wife.. Incubus and succubus demons, Incubus is a demon in male form who lies upon a sleeping woman in order to have sexual intercourse with the woman.

Succubus is the female counterpart; These spirits are home wreckers, One may awaken to feel as if they have actually been engaged in the act of lovemaking Or say that they've had a wet dream because it can seem so real, But its actually spiritual Sex. These demons can even take on the face of an ex lover, cause Misfortune and Miscarriage, Masturbation will invite these spirits into one life, they can be picked up at bars and night clubs, They will lay clam to a person and will not let the person have a lasting or Loving relationship they will reek total havoc and marital confusion until the person your planing to marry or get to know better is out of your life completely , And most often the victim never knew what went wrong, Always wondering " why can't I ever keep a relationship "what's wrong with me? These spirits are joined at the hip to make ones life miserable and very unhappy they bring failure ..."this is a serious matter. Anything sexual In the demonic realm will always belong to the water kingdom.

Queen of the coast spirits, Jezebel Marine Woman who are not even real woman, their on assignment to destroy the Men of God especially those who have been called to Pastor a Church.

It's so much here that I could literately stay on this topic two hrs or more

There are Marine Dedications where people dedicate their children to the water spirits, and when the child turns a certain age those spirits will call for the child to return to the waters and be given it's assignment to carry out upon the earth, what the child was formerly initiated for and return them back to their families. Marine Weddings are done where Woman and Men actually Marry these spirits with an Marine Alter, And refuse the love of a natural Man or Woman.

*** Stars are the currency of the Marine Kingdom. Stolen Star Currency ..."We all have a star..Stars can be and are stolen from certain ones and given to the ones that have sold their souls to Satan.. Some of us have really bright Stars that is Why Famous People are referred to as Stars. Those of us that have really bright stars, satanic agents target us desperately eager to throw us to the ground. We can reclaim our star and all of our stolen treasures from this evil Kingdom of course through the power of Jesus Christ and his blood that was ahead on carvery for the remission of our sins. So now that we have been made aware we can pray over our Children and Grandchildren in this area,

Cover their Stars in the Blood of Jesus Christ. Pregnancy is one way that Witches Initate, Scouts for Unborn Children; by touching and rubbing the belly's of A Pregnant Women.. they mark the child while rubbing and touching the mother for a way later time in their life's the pull will come upon to practice evil and the witch that was rubbing the mother will get the credit for it and move up in the satanic ranks if He or She joins. Witches know and use hand,& finger coded signals;masons occultists, gang members, and many other groups of people use secret hand signals, hand shakes, and grips to secretly signal.

Proverbs 6:12 -15 Speaks of a wicked Man A naughty person walking with a forward mouth he winketh with his eyes he speaketh with his feet he teacheth with his fingers forwardness is in his heart he deviseth mischief continually he soweth discord... KJV... While jollying around with you but the entire time their up to no good" their distracting you with fictitious laughter and rubbing Your Belly with both hands and cursing your unborn fetus at the same time and you're totally unaware of what is taking place, So what happens next?" is that when your Child Turns 10 or 11 years old he or she begins to go astray and become controllable A Monster! And you have No idea where or what to do. So when pregnant don't show your stomach's cover them up" don't take pictures with your Pregnant belly exposed for social Media" or Ware clothes that expose your Pregnant Belly in public..Isiah 3:12 Say's Children shall be their Oppressors .

Still talking about the Marine Kingdom..

Spiritual Containers are beholding many peoples blessing; Satanic Jars Peoples destinies and Souls are caged and placed inside jars along with a host of other things and thrown into the sea or some river.. "Water Spirits People go to them to find growth and multiply in worldly things; its a fact that in order for something to grow it needs water nourishment one of the four elements ..Water "what I've learned about the four elements while doing research for this book... fire, air, water, and earth, were the first development from the first matter; each of these elements combines two of the four primary qualities which exist in all things – hot, cold, wet, dry, fire is hot and dry, air is hot and wet, water is cold and wet, earth is cold and dry, everything is made of the four elements and the differences between objects or materials are caused by the differing proportions in which the elements are combined in them.. "Said all that to say that if one of the qualities of an element is altered it turns into a different element; when fire which is hot and dry loses it's heat it becomes cold and dry and changes into earth becoming ash' when water which is cold and wet is heated it becomes hot and wet and changes into air giving off vapor.. so" this made me to wonder what is the element in Witchcraft In Occult Magic, In all its forms I'm looking for the main ingredient that makes Witches Fly So I can pull the plug! I'm studying and writing at the same time as I move along here with this book, the main element In Witchcraft is the Python Anytime witchcraft is on the seen Python is right there, Python itself is the spirit of divination.

I may have to sell it out of the trunk of my van.. to get it to the people, the first book I wrote (Warfare Strategies) was published by a woman who pretended to be all about him (Jesus) later I find out that this person was a phoney she acted as if she cared so much for me and my family I was fooled big time by her. I do Love her still and learned so many great things from her. I couldn't understand for all that she thought me about God "why was I feeling her presence in my home sometimes, and why was my book not selling on amazon or anyplace for that matter" so I begin to seek the lord for three whole days I prayed asking God" what is the deal Lord ? I send her our tithes, we texted each other often.. had lot's of laughs even talked about relocating to her city well" we did" and it was a disaster!" and very short lived ... "well anyway standing at the kitchen sink in My home in Indianapolis I heard the Lord say" ...("She's Playing A Roll!) Just like that" She hated me couldn't stand me in her heart.. And "Oh how I loved her! I always wanted a spiritual Mother someone to teach me spiritual things help me to mature and grow in the Lord even if I had to buy one..I was like that little bird in the little Children's story book who went around to all the wrong animals asking are you My Mother? But anyway while editing the book she telephone me one day and ask " do you want your photo on the book.. I asked what do you think? She said yes I would" do you have one?" she asked "I said yes I'll mail it to you, she lived and pastored a church two hrs away from where I lived at that time. So I immediately put the photo into the us mail; excited about my first little book well as time went on the photo was never returned to me. She told me I apologize to you " My daughter cleans up for me' and she must have thrown it away" because I can't find it anywhere.. I am sorry" she said..'' My husband Said I don't believe that" but Me I said well why would she lie about something like that"?? and I just went on with my life, one night about a year or so later while at a deliverance Meeting, the Ministering Woman told me that theirs a woman that has your picture; talking about (me) inside a pentagram and is praying witchcraft prayers over it chanting over it" ... "Who did you give a picture of yourself to? She also told me that Christ has his foot placed over it he's covering it with his foot... glory be to God" Religious Deception is on the rise. I have quite a few stories I can tell about, people who've I've encountered throughout the years who are in the Lord's house claiming that they are children of God but are NOT! They are children of the devil Revelation 2:9

Nothing aggravates me more than this! I have to be honest ..Witches in the house of the Lord working and holding office". Lets take a look at Witches, I've been collecting information on witches for quite some time I know at lease ten years or more... Everywhere I'd go, Church, Marketplace,Children School, Work Place, I'd run into Witches Now I know that Jesus Loves Them because he said in his word that he wishes that No One would Parrish... 2 Peter 3:9

Witches Mark

Witches & Wizards will a lot of times have edifying marks like moles,warts other stains and scratches, blue and red dots on their skin and to top it off" they'll will always have an odor that cannot be washed away or perfumed over it will always be there.

There are different levels in the demonic realm depending on how deep one want's to get involved; There are some Witches that continue in Church because of their spouses and families members, not knowing their big little Secret. Closet Witches... I heard it said by one closet Witch that she hates when Sunday comes because she has to go to church" she feels like an island while sitting among the other saints" Well I was just grateful that she wasn't trying to preach or teach Sunday School. She said she believes in Jesus but he is not the right choice for her, as long as she treats nature well she is worshiping the divine she believes.. were going to take a long look into some of the characteristics that identify witches.. <u>Now" let me add NOT ALWAYS THE CASE" in every person let the holy spirit lead you and be your guide to judgment; here are some signs one witch says to look for:</u>

- they are naturally drawn to nature love the outside plants animals getting hands dirty.
- love animals, they feel more comfortable with animals then people.
- they are drawn to the moon sit and stare at the moon interested in all its cycles and the energy of it.
- drawn to the healing arts they prefer alternative medicine over traditional medicine they believe in natural healing and believe that they themselves are a healer.
- they love anything involving the occult occultic related things

they love storms rain collecting rain water.

Going vegan.. overboard concerning what they are eating.

There are many categories of witchcraft and people who walk on this left hand path of witchyness (my word) Glory be to God after reading this book we will know the signs when a witch is among us.. some people say that there are good witches and bad witches I can't put good and Witch into the same sentence .. God said suffer a witch not to live... key word (WITCH) He did not any witch is alright with him... white ones, blue ones, black ones, here are 9 different characteristics types of Witches that I came across while studying and I think there are at lease 2 more the moon witch and the sea witch I have yet to study about these other ones. I must remind me to do so. These satanists infest ever part and level of our society, the poor and the rich, they can be Male or Female; they usually have high iqs their also really good talkers too" sale snow to an Eskimo they lead double lives, they'll transform themselves into an angels of light and ministers of righteousness at the drop of a hat, mostly of all of them attend a local christian church somewhere they come on as really good citizens and they love civic activities this all done as COVER UP! And they are better than good at it.

#1  augury witch – similar to a shaman she or he helps direct those on spiritual quest by interpreting the signs and symbols the traveler encounters. The term comes from augurs, whose function was not to tell the future but to discover whether or not the gods approved of a proposed coarse of action by interpreting signs or omen such as the appearance of animals sacred to the gods they believe their gifts is prophecy and not divination.. Shakespeare witches appear as augury witches.

# 2 ceremonial witch. One who combines both the practices of witchcraft and ceremonial magic, they use a combination of things drawn from old ways they will call upon a ecclectic band of spiritual

entities leaning towards archetypal figures. They are more spiritual centered using an earth centered path with focus on the feminine divine within.

#3 Eclectic Witch

This one has an individual approach they choose from many different traditions for whatever works best for them, a little bit of this a little bit of that.

#4 Faery Witch

An eclectic who seeks to commune with faery folk and nature spirits they have no organizations or tradition.

# 5 The Green Witch

Mother nature use of use natural items, magic through mother nature and using earth energies.

# 6 The Hedge Witch

Earth base spirituality these are the ones who engage in spirit flight better known as astral projection journey into the outter world they are said to be very powerful midwifes and healers a bird of one kind or another is usually associated with the hedge witch most commonly the raven and the goose they work more with the dark side.

#7 Hereditary Witch

Known as a family tradition witches keep the old ways they've been thought blood magic. Believes strong in keeping the family together the family bloodline.

#8 The Kitchen Witch who uses the tools at hand to work their spells. It's more than cooking, although they love to cook and make things for home. they find the scared in everyday tast it's an increasingly popular type of witchcraft. They also work the energies of nature to make home a secure place.

#9 Solitary Witch this is one who practices alone without a coven and without following any particular tradition, they are a legend among other witches because they have practiced for a lifetime they have passed puberty "so to speak.

Water Witch

They tend to work with spirits that are associated with the water and worship goddesses born of the waves, Water Witchcraft is a "genre" of witchcraft that honors and derives its power from the water.

Theses Witches do spells and rituals! You may find a Sea Witch drawing signals in the sand or collecting sea water! You may find a River Witch meditating in a quite space under low hanging trees over a rippling river. Flowers are often found on the beach, remnants of a ritual that was performed there before, however they can often be problematic,

Witches in general tend to have many boxes, bags, and bottles! But Water Witches tend to have more bottles and jars than anything! A witch's cabinet is just as unique as the witch varying with their tradition and path. In it you may find various jars of water including, ocean water, muddy water, rain water, full moon water, holy water, water from various sacred springs and local water sources, Florida water, war water, floral essences, gem essences and other strange watery concoctions!

Chances are that they will have a shrine or altar space that is watery in nature or even dedicated to the water or a water god/ess. Or perhaps a collection of prized sea shells intermingled with candles that are more to you than decoration.

Now lets take a look at some of the things they do.. Witches are sneaky and will take full advantage of a person who is ignorant of their devices, They cannot read a persons mind, but will definitely test their luck at trying to place a spell, hex curse on someone by calling up demons and sending them to the person to work havoc in their lives, and cause the person to loose things all spells are accomplished by demons even the so called good ones" in My first book warfare strategies I tell about the testimony of a delivered witch doctor that has now turned her life over to Christ Jesus, She said that it is an expiration date to all witchcraft spells and curses.. that's why people keep running back and forth she said they call this the hip hop looking for a witchdoctor that has stronger charms.

Older powerful witches will communicate with demons directly in the spirit world through their guiding spirit (they call it) like we children of God have the Holy Spirit Satan is a copy cat he can't create but only duplicate. But this guiding spirit is a demon that the witch will ask to come and live inside her or him for the purpose of having all sorts of occult skills and powers and communication with other demons.

They make things like fetishes, talisman, amulets and incorporate things like their enemies hair, fingernails blood into whatever fetish their making things that hold a persons DNA is a treasure to them.. also they can be objects that can be worn on the body or hung over the door of a house office etc.

All this is the work of Satan which God strictly forbids.

Blood: called the river of life, Is sacred to all evil workers blood is used to bind oaths and drink (Isaiah 66:17 )this abominable practice is taken up in the brotherhood, also either by mingling or in signing satanic contracts. They believe that a blood oath is inviolate, there is such a thing called a devil's pack that is always signed in blood, making an agreement between the individual and the devil; "But the Blood of Jesus can and will annihilate and utterly destroy this agreement when one accepts Jesus Christ, the precious blood of Jesus wipes it all out. Anyway they believe a few drops of a person's blood is used in the magical charms and spells is sprinkled in potions is said to give the witch or wizard power over that person don't be careless with any blood that comes from your body, blood that comes from your body can be used in love spells also don't be careless with the disposal of sanitary napkins or any fluid that comes from your body I personally had a woman at a place of employment one time " she heard me blowing my nose and sneezing and she was actually following me around with the waist basket she kept offering it to me, stretching it out" making a juster for me to drop the dirty tissue inside ; I went into the restroom and flushed it." and I guess your saying what in the word was she going to do with someone's nasty tissue well for one ... place it upon a satanic alter as an representation of me she wanted to curse me perhaps bar me from the job just whatever her little evil mind was thinking, Cigarettes butts too can be used" I recall when I use to smoke cigerrettes I was at my boyfriends home visiting and I had been there over 3 hours watching movies eating, drinking, drinking alcohol at that time in My life.. "so I know," I was smoking more than My usual one or two cigarette here and there, well it dawn on me to look into the ashtray, and it was only a few butts in there!" no one had emptied it'.. OK I know I've been drinking but I'm not Crazy "this guy was taking My used cigarette butts because My saliva My (DNA) was on them; doing evil rituals over them, "these crazy people like to place things on their satanic evil alters, and do satanic burials, where they bury stuff in the earth, and burn things in caldrons they also use animal blood in rituals they will kill an animal for this purpose It could be the family pet, once they've become this satanist you don't know them any more if it's your own child BE careful with them "especially if Mom ,Dad, or anyone in the home is a true christian stay alert" and watch your step when their around ."I'm not saying by no means give up on them ..."do keep praying for them, but do watch as well as pray, especially if they live in the house with you, I'd say guard your bedroom when your not there Lock it up! Open Drinks in the fridge, instant coffee, creamer anything you use on a daily basis too", Pay attention to how your feeling after eating and drinking when their around or been around, pay attention the the atmosphere, Don't get caught up in "Oh that's just "My Son, My Daughter Sister Brother Mother" etc Don't be deceived.. By fake tears and fake hugs,when they've become committed to these cult groups they loose all emotions of love and compassion and become cruel people some have been programmed personalities have been split and they've been taken captive to do the will of Satan, they may even actually have a handler . That trains them to do the job and preform rituals which include how to use knifes, guns, how to speak in other languages, even martial arts, at some point they'll disappear for a few day's for reprogramming and training this stuff is so serious to them ... they may even come up hurt from time to time from having to participate in a fight with other coven kids to be tested of strength and their supernatural abilities... demonic fighting... spirituality and physically

REMEMBER it's the members of our own household...

"If they have given their life to Jesus they will tell you things that were dark secrets occult extremely secretive things about the kingdom of darkness that took place while on the inside" if they remain quiet and won't talk they have NOT Renounce Satan and it's kingdom of darkness they may appear weak and submissive as if ready to give the person that's trying to help them get free from the demonic chains control over them and their lives.. Don't be fooled for a moment, they are highly trained and programmed empowered to deceived and can run circles around us normal people, they will play you like a fiddle, they are quick and strong they are always watching too.. they'll being seeing you without you seeing them; in Jesus name command their 3rd eye to be closed in Jesus Name... "I read that punishment and pain awaits if they don't accomplish their tast well.

Corinthians 2:11..Say's

Lest Satan should get an advantage of us: for we are not ignorant of his devices. (Don't be outwitted) kjv

Many of them are church goer's and devil worshipers at the same time, they can go to church but the church dose not have any impact on them

Their mission is to destroy the true saints of God and bring down the churches.

Some assignments may be to infiltrate the church, they start by being a fake christian and bring compromise to the people there, or the coven wants to get in far enough so they can gain access to the building to get inside to perform rituals and ruin the leadership

**Daniel 11:31 King James Version (KJV**

And arms shall stand on his part, and they shall pollute the sanctuary of strength, and shall take away the daily sacrifice, and they shall place the abomination that maketh desolate.

Here are a few things to rebuke in prayer when praying against Witches, Wizards, Satanist, Let me also Add:

I have had people say that they are to afraid to pray against these satanic workers for fear of retaliation... TIP

After-wards Cut the cords and the links all tracks that would lead back to you (me) with the FIRE of the holy spirit the refiners FIRE!!!

Remember the story of Hansel and Gretel... Hansel dropped the breadcrumbs to find he and Gretel's way back home after his Father left him and his frighten little sister alone in the woods because they were eating to much.

Well I like to use this story of how the backlash returns to us..

the breadcrumbs we dropped in prayer gives the enemy a b-line to us

but when I Cut and Burn the spiritual cords and links the conection is gone" I can literally feel the connection when it loosens from me, also say this after you've shared some spiritual advice.

ANNIHILATE:

Their Strategies, Tools, And Evil Wisdom.

Circles ... They like to put things inside a Circle someones photo.

Hexagrams

Pentagrams

Triangles

7 day cruses

Moon cycles

And always but always" their concentration they can't function without it.

Demons and witches' they specialize in the same thing to bring someone down, witches" they think they are controlling the demons but the demons are really controlling them.

Don't reveal to much about what you know, this will open the door for attack against you, They can be paranoid so don't talk to much about what you know .They rely on ones ignorance, Witches have super sneakiness ..I can recall when I had a guest at my home, visiting from out of town for a few day's and every morning she would come to my bedroom door holding her toothbrush in hand telling me, that she forgot her toothpaste.. I'd point to the bathroom it's in there "id nicely say.. You're welcome to it, toothpaste is something one use's everyday..My husband and Myself ..If I were secretly out to cause havoc in someone's home marriage etc.. they both use the toothpaste.. (techniques)...

Don't give place to the devil Look,

Watch Them Dogs Philippians 3:2.. I am sending you out like sheep among wolves; therefore be as shrewd as snakes and as innocent as doves. Matthew 10:16

Genesis 3:1

Now the serpent was more crafty than any beast of the field that the LORD God had made. And he said to the woman, "Did God really say, 'You must not eat of any tree in the garden?'"

Root Doctors ... Are widely sought after by their clients in a quiet hush hush way, due to being shunned, altho some like to be shunned they find it a honer, for instance like the body of Christ face's percussion ... anyway they are well respected members of their churches and communities people will travel many miles to consult with one of these people over and over again and pay them top dollar for their services.

This is very real, this is not something that is child's play or a ferry tail the more we see the rebellion against God, in the world the More Witchcraft will grow, and assume to overthrow us; it's deep within the Government offices and systems, education systems, and we don't even have to mention Arts and Entertainment, T.V, and Film, Social Media, and the Medical field, there are More Doctors and Nurses that are involved in the Secret Occult Society today than you can ever, Imagine doing things you could never Imagine doing, Killing newborn babies for Satanic Rituals these Mothers become pregnant only for this one purpose, to offer up their babies for this cause to sacrifice them, they see this as a high honor to Satan and the kingdom of darkness; the expecting Mother stay's out of sight or perhaps may be sent away to another town or state and is provided for until time for delivery. There's no record of a doctor's visit they have their own medical doctors inside the occult. This reminds me of something My Dear Old Grandmother use to say"... "Anything you got to hide and do it, " Now You know Your doing wrong in most cases" (she was from the south).

Points Of Contact:

To establish an evil point of contact the evil worker will need and try to get some type of symbolic object Or Clothing or Jewelry in your Home, Car, Office, anywhere that you will be at some point of time, they can give you a gift for your home or office.. how about a nice Vase or a Plant or a Candy Dish, also Money but the gift for your home or office is something the person will always have with them like a key chain the goal is to give something that the person will keep...The evil Worker will spiritually enhance the gift with a demonic charge with the aim of enslaving and establishing a contact between the unsuspecting victims; Some have been known to just drop by for a visit and leave a gift without the person even knowing it.. It's a shame when you feel that you need to check the under the seat where the person sat after they have gone... One Woman's Shared that she had a guest that ask to use the ladies room and while inside the restroom she cut's a piece of the bathroom rug to take back to her demonic Altar;

A Pastor from Ohio tells that a Woman came to his Church in the middle of the day upset about problems within her Marriage , Hysterically Crying in the lobby to the point he came out of his office to see what was all the fuss, Oh how she just needed to see the Pastor.. Long story short she left him an unknown gift stuff down inside the couch where she sat.

**Micah 2:1 Woe to those who plan iniquity, to those who plot evil on ...b**

New International Version Woe to those who plan iniquity, to those who plot evil on their beds! At morning's light they carry it out because it is in their power to do it. New Living Translation What sorrow awaits you who lie awake at night, thinking up evil plans. You rise at dawn and hurry to carry them out, simply because you ...

These evil Workers set up various types of entrapment's and avenues of destruction through ways they can easily establish a forced entry point with unsuspecting victims, their opportunist they exploits circumstances to gain immediate advantage; they will also create a situation that will get them in.. They watch and study you from a distance, What you eat, Soda Pop you like then, the evil worker with the evil agenda will bring you some of your favorite after it's been sent through the enslaving process to take the unsuspecting person captive and gain control over them. .

New International Version: They covet fields and seize them, and houses, and take them. They defraud people of their homes, they rob them of their inheritance. When you want a piece of land, you find a way to seize it. When you want someone's house, you take it by fraud and violence. Micah 2:3-4

people who seek out demons are hungry for power but they do so in ignorance and become entrapped and held in bondage to Satan. If you or someone you know has made a pact with the devil, The first order of business is to renounce it, take back the words spoken.. When the vow was made and the oath was taken whatever words were spoken at that time.. Declare them null and void and say" it has no more power over Bill or Bobby's life in Jesus Name. I pray a total cleansing over his or her body and complete purification from whatever potion they partook of I place the blood of Jesus Over it..Now

Spirits are subject to us, we need to know how to fight and not blame God all the time for what we're going through, You remember that one girl on the block when if you got into it with her you'd have to fight all day long" You be like dag, OK.. that's how We need to be with the enemy keep that joker up against the wall, There are two things the devil can't stand that is the name of Jesus and the Blood of Jesus, Own our own Satan is to strong and wise it's the name of Jesus Christ that's greater than Satan's Power; Satan's power is limited But Jesus' is not.

Satan can not be everywhere at all times but Jesus is all seeing all knowing almighty God, Who will leave your enemies in a state of confusion.

Four Corners: These are hiding places for those that lay around; snares inside corners of a place house, office building just where ever they want to bind up through demonic control witchcraft.

Among My people are found wicked Men they lay wait, as he that setteth snares; they set a trap, to catch Men . As a cage is full of birds so are their houses full of deceit: therefore they are become great ,and waxen rich.. Jeremiah 5:26

Meaning they lurk privily for the innocent without cause and do evil

While Men slept the enemy came and sewed tares among the wheat.. Matthew 13:25 ..(While he was unaware)

Arise, and let us go by night, and let us destroy her palaces.. Jeremiah 6:5

There are some people that just have an ever renewing fresh supply of wickedness for each new day. Now we kinda know that it's not them the person, but it's the spirit, the evil spirit that the person has yielded themselves unto. We are human, and all kinds of thoughts do inter into our minds, but we must cast them down, not give into them or play with them in our minds. 2Corinthians 10:5 (KJV) Say's

Casting down imaginations, and every high thing that exalteth itself against the knowledge of God, and bringing into captivity every thought to the obedience of Christ; so these thoughts will come to mind, evil thoughts, ungodly thoughts, If we do not cast down vain thinking we will become transformed by them creating a stronghold in our minds; And this stronghold will create opposition to the work of the Gospel that you've been called to live and preach. After casting the vain thought down replace it with the fresh rewed word of God in that place example... thought comes to Mind" wonder what it's like to have Sex with his Wife?

OK" You say "I rebuke that thought.. find scripture, the bible says let every Man have his own Wife. KJV

Nevertheless, *to avoid* fornication, let every man have his own wife, and let every woman have her own husband.2 corinthians7;2

"After all, after we have preached to others we ourselves don't want to become a castaway.

1 Thessalonians 4:4

each of you must know how to control his own body in holiness and honor,

Ask God to expose all who are involved, and to know why; attack their power base with fire, crush their protection, and pray to cut off their unity.

You can destroy your enemy if you have enough information and likewise.

Satanic Arrows: Evil Exchanges: Evil Altars: Time release Demons:

I have Often wondered about many things, I have so many things I want to make known I'm praying as I type because the enemy is trying to attack me with confusion I have the information inside my head but it want's to jam up.

I have seen as I'm sure you have to, Witches praying over people breaking curses; didn't know at that time they were witches, but after the Holy Spirit reviled it.. questions began to arise" You think back on things and be like "well Lord how can a witch cast out a demon..? How can Satan cast out Satan? "and break curses off of people .. I've seen it done right in the church. and later find out that the person is a Witch or Warlock "how can a Witch be working in deliverance? How Lord?" This puzzled me for Many day's I kept praying requiring about it; studying everything;.. In the kingdom of darkness there is rank, when a demonic spell is placed on a person by an evil worker, that summons demons, another evil worker that is stronger and that has more power in the demonic realm than the one that place the spell in the beginning is able to remove the curse, and be looked upon as an angel of light. The Demonic realm respect's power.

Charms/Amulets These are very Important to these witch doctors and their clients, They make evil charms for people to ware or carry about with them, they can have them placed inside their bodies through swallowing or making an incision ,it may for sure have words written upon it and spoken over it, A spell.. I met one lady that had hers in her hair, she never knew that I knew' for the holy spirit had reviled it to me;

These Demonic Charms can be bracelets Jewelry sewed into something that is carried or worn everyday, for instance a Mans Belt, inside a Shoe Or a Jacket/ Coat a Woman's Purse Or as I said earlier placed inside their bodies.

These Charms are so important to them they believe inside the charm is where the power lies and the demons are able to contact them; the ones that have them placed inside their bodies, they say that the charms gives them more demonic wisdom,.. wisdom to create, create and invent evil ideas It Enhances their evil intelligence even the more and to fit themselves into whole thing to become one with the charm, Here's the thing", the Bible says that Satan comes too ...Steal, Kill and Dis troy John 10;10 but Christ came to give us life and give it more abundantly anything the enemy gives is a set up and a trap to ruin your life, in the end, things will always be much worse than at it's beginning don't get into any covenant with the kingdom of darkness; he hates God and the children of God; I read that a woman testified about how an anxious and exhausted Mother came to see her searching for a way to get her Son into this Prestigious ivy league Collage, her son didn't have the grade point average he needed to attend this up scale school, and She was worried, and not taking NO for an answer ,worried that her son might not be excepted like his first cousin whom she was the aunt too.. The evil worker stated that after the anxious Mother pays the fee and go's away, The evil worker recalls how she can remember the demons" hysterically laughing and laughing and laughing at the Mother calling the anxious Mother a foolish woman, because she just sold her Son to the devil. "He will be excepted into the prestigious School But- But he will commits suicide: He will never graduate! the evil spirits shouted over and over again while laughing.. Id like to tell you that the mother found Jesus in time and the evil wishes of the demons did not come to pass, unfortunately "I don't know the outcome to this story... But my point is that Satan will never give You or Me anything without an evil price attached to it, he's not going to let anyone stand with a happy and Joyous heart at the end.. if he has his evil way. People come and go to these evil workers looking for healing, Well if someone has pain in the arm area , a demonic healing will remove the pain from the arm only to send it to the stomach with only much worse symptoms... No one will ever stand with the victory... thoe your rich you will never enjoy it, thoe your Married You will never know or feel the real true genuine God given Love in the Marriage and plus Jesus is not obligated to fight for that Marriage because after all he did not put it together, It's not covered or protected under his blood.

A Newlywed Couple after 4 years of Marriage and 3 months of going through diagnostic testing and treatments with fertility Doctors she was at wits end with being unsuccessful in pregnancy, she tried everything to no avail still no children, just balances due owed to various fertility clients though out the City; embarrassed by the struggle and the whispering..When they say to you, "Consult the mediums and the spiritists who whisper and mutter," should not a people consult their God? Should they consult the dead on behalf of the living?**Isaiaih 8:19 ASV**

**Toni** loved her Husband very much and wanted nothing more than to reward him with a beautiful baby girl, his hearts desire to give him the wonderful news that they were going to soon be parents..She went to the dark side for help,... Woe to those who go down to Egypt for help and rely on horses and trust in chariots.. Isaiah 31:1...kjv

A month later Toni was Pregnant ! And the baby was born with all kinds of birth defects and health problems and had to have multiples surgeries at two and three months old and the child did not live.. such sad heartbreaking news.. Satan has no love or compassion only trickery. When a person go's to inquire of these evil workers what is happening is they take the destines of a child or a family member, and as you engaging in the ritual the person is also engaging in an exchange. It's the system of Witchcraft manipulation.

Don't be deceived God is not Mocked what soever a Man soweth that shall he shall also reap.. Galatians 6:7-9 kjv

Another evil tool satanic workers use is placing nails into things, to hold things in a certain place : To hold people down, in place, so that they cannot move or advance in life, Or to hold things together, like a relationship.. I have a family Member when I would visit her, I would sometimes see an old crusty nail down around her apartment door, that see never saw' or just didn't;t notice and even if she did, she had no idea, Now there were times I'd just remove the nail" but a few day's later the nail was back; so I finally decided to make her aware of My findings,I told her I don't want to sound like im'a lil Touched each time I see a nail.." I do realize... NOT ALWAYS THE CASE. I didin't have a case of paranoia or suffering from mental illness... "She Immediately begin to agree with Me, that I was on the Right street with this information because she had been wondering about some things concerning this new boyfriend that she couldn't seem to shake..

She believed that Sam was putting the nail there to hold his relationship with her in place.

Had a Pastor friend that I really liked, I preached at her church a few times altho "I don't think I'm a Preacher, "I Spoke at her Church," Yeah" that sounds better... So anyway after service was over one Saturday evening hanging around recapping on the powerful service we just endured, I was in motion to leave, I stooped at the bottom of the three small steps, for a last few words while standing there still talking, but bringing it to a close, I asked her hay" Lu" do you ever check around your door area?"as I was asking, I began to look around in search and underneath the last step.. I reach down and Picked up the largest old rusty nail I'd ever seen..I wish you could have seen the look on her face... She had Placed that nail there under that step herself!" yes" so that her members would not leave" her Church.." in her mind that was to hold the people down so that they wouldn't her leave her Church.." can you Image what else is she might be doing?"

A lady that I knew who had seem to be interested in learning about spiritual warfare she and I had become telephone friends we lived in different states she would be present on every conference call I did, and would keep me encouraged and uplifted which is good when God has called you to this type of Ministering you" know some one who can vouch "No she's not Crazy "I know her she's alright; there is a thin thread between the divine and the demonic." Well one day this young Lady we'll call her Tina.. Tina sent me a text Message where she had taken a picture Of an Old long Rusty Nail that look like it had been put through the fire, burned and coded with something and burned again it was ugly to look at; anyway she sent me this picture in a text Message telling Me how she found this old nail down by her front step that Morning, asking me to take a look at it, and did I think it was Witchcraft"? Well I assured her that I felt like it was so.. but I didin't erase the text out of My Phone I continued to carry it along with Me everywhere I went, as time past on "I Forgot that I even had the text in My Phone; She knew exactly what she was doing she had sent that text to Me as a curse for Me It was her point of contact.. I was at Work started feeling like I was about to go insane this particular day steped away from my work area went into a little room and prayed the heavenly father brought my cellular phone to my attention, and I pulled it out look it over and remembered the picture of the nail, so I Immediately deleted the entire text log everything she'd ever sent. "For thus the LORD of hosts, the God of Israel, Do not let your prophets who are in your midst and your diviners deceive you, and do not listen to the dreams which they dream. 9'For they prophesy falsely to you in My name; I have not sent them,' declares the LORD....

New American Standard B Jeremiah 29:8

In that day, saith the LORD of hosts, shall the nail that is fastened in the sure place be removed, and be cut down, and fall; and the burden that *was* upon it shall be cut off: for the LORD hath spoken *it*. Isaiah:22:25

Before a witchdoctor performs a ritual on their altar that alter requires a sacrifice; it could be an Animal, Someone's bodily fluids, bodily hairs pubic, nail clippings or their strongest call... BLOOD' just anything with the persons personal life matter attach to it ..DNA.. no altar will deliver for them the evil priest working at that altar without a sacrifice.

A satanic altar is a place designed for offerings and sacrifices to Satan and his demons in order to appease them or to make a request for their assistance to do something.

It's also a place where blood is shed either animals or humans, I read some place that it is a satanic dining table; it's a place of spiritual exchange. exchange is made, they use their alters to store their charms; they report to their alters first thing in the morning to get information for their day, they have bottles sitting around with fake labels attached to them. I wish to make known all the secrets of the enemy to the body of Christ the More knowledgeable we are the better we fight! The better we hold our ground.

Charms and Alters are so very important to these evil workers when you and I attack thees bases in prayer praise the Lord" you have latterly sent a cannon ball into their mist. Glory Be To God! I Have some prayer points at the end of this topic. The word of the Lord say's that we are to pray against these satanic altars they shall be rent and the ashes poured out that were upon it. And, behold, there came a man of God out of Judah by the word of the Lord unto Bethel: and Jeroboam stood by the altar to burn incense.

And he cried against the altar in the word of the Lord, and said, O altar, altar, thus saith the Lord; Behold, a child shall be born unto the house of David, Josiah by name; and upon thee shall he offer the priests of the high places that burn incense upon thee, and Men's bones shall be burnt upon thee.

And he gave a sign the same day, saying, This is the sign which the Lord hath spoken; Behold, the altar shall be rent, and the ashes that are upon it shall be poured out.

And it came to pass, when king Jeroboam heard the saying of the man of God, which had cried against the altar in Bethel, that he put forth his hand from the altar, saying, Lay hold on him. And his hand, which he put forth against him, dried up, so that he could not pull it in again to him.

The altar also was rent, and the ashes poured out from the altar, according to the sign which the man of God had given by the word of the Lord... 1kings 13:1-5 kjv

Altars have a what is called a 3$^{rd}$ eye for monitoring they also speak shut their eyes and silence them pray that they be blinded by the holy ghost fire and forbid them to speak or reveal any information concerning you, silence them in Jesus mighty Name Amen.

**Monitoring Spirit** is a weapon of witchcraft attack that manipulates its victim to disrupt his life, by making him miss his blessings, vulnerable to ill-luck, failure and frustration. The plight of the victim of **monitoring spirit** can be explained as that of a person that has a rope tied to one of his legs... The Guardian Nigeria Magazine.

Prayer points Against: Altars/ Charms

When a person takes someone's hair, nails clothing, anything that comes off the body to the evil worker it is used for a point of contact something that connects you (the victim) with that alter; they are looking for something that identifies you (the victim) that ties you with that alter, identification comes by your blood or a garment which is what every alter needs and wants mostly is blood but the next best thing is hair nail clippings or worn clothes unwashed or a photo. It's noted that after being attached to an evil alter even if the person travels up to 10,000 miles the evil alter can still locate the person because it's like the law having your finger print, It stays on file the evil alter has the same mandate the demonic spirits ties one to that particular alter the demonic spirits travel right along with the person.

Please have NO FEAR.. Greater is he who is in YOU than He who is in the World.. Jesus Christ has overcome the World. This is just information to help us survive, in this Way Beyond Wicked World, We have to live in, and We cannot continue to shut our eyes and ears to what's going around us, We must be WISE as a Serpent.

Matthew 10:16 King James Version (KJV)

Behold, I send you forth as sheep in the midst of wolves: be ye therefore wise as serpents, and harmless as doves.

Matthew 10:16 King James Version (KJV)

Behold, I send you forth as sheep in the midst of wolves: be ye therefore wise as serpents, and harmless as doves.

I Must Repeat Sants Children Of The Most High God Again

Be Not Afraid:

All of creation is waiting on Us, The Sons of God to rise up and put things back in order, We have the power and authority to do so we sit in heavenly places with Christ Jesus.

3 Defend the poor and fatherless: do justice to the afflicted and needy.

4 Deliver the poor and needy: rid them out of the hand of the wicked.

5 They know not, neither will they understand; they walk on in darkness: all the foundations of the earth are out of course. Psalms 82:3-5..kjv

Psalms 82 say's deliver the poor and needy: rid them out of the hand of the Wicked, I believe God is talking to us here. . The know not, neither will they understand, they walk on in darkness, but look at verse 5.. All The Foundations Of The Earth Are Out Of Coarse.. This is because the children of God has not raised UP! All we have to do is walk in our God given authority. Satan left Jesus for a season which means he'll be coming back again, there will always be attacks, Always" and by what You don't know can destroy you. But that will not be the case because you now have within your reach a wealth of Information. The enemy has the ability to gain access in your life through ignorance.. as you well know our enemy is spiritual and must be fought on a spiritual battle ground.. He's not fought with natural means & weapons..

OK back to the alters..

You become a Force to be wreaking with when you have knowledge about these altars and know how to dismantle them.

-Annihilate them and the priest working It. Rebuke anything that they have in their satanic register. Rebuke and cancel any situation they are working to create to gain an entry and get a label and Id for their alter. They create situations for you to come to them.

Witchcraft systems: be on the lookout for them.

Alters ,charms, dream pollution, contamination

- I pray that every satanic alter raised up against Me be pulled down and overthrown
- Every evil exchange I curse with Fire
- I cover your evil alter with the blood of Jesus
- Curse the seat that their sitting in.
- Curse their wands, tools, goblets candles, knifes, etc

Another thing to be knowledgeable about is stones.

Job 5:23 King James Version (KJV)

For thou shalt be in league with the stones of the field: and the beasts of the field shall be at peace with thee.

These people lay stones, rocks Intended to paralyze someone's progress they set snares one thing I've learn is that they use the most, are natural things, so you won't take notice ;but these are not just any old stones they pray evil prayers over them incantations and then bring them and place them around the area where their target victim lives, works, parked their, car to hold down their targeted victim.

Church Witches.. They need something to hide behind, like their gift or a title or a class their teaching, I heard one woman say.." they always want to teach the children. there's something that they are hiding that cannot be seen on the surface, as we know, "witchcraft is manipulation and control when its evident in the church, the rider of the horse always wants to have something going on and with all of the attention on them, and you'll feel funny if your not a part of it, whatever their doing this month; the funny feeling is the demonic pull, their pulling you to come run and get engulfed after them and what their presenting.. You know that something is wrong but can't seem to put your finger on it.." After all they are in church every week, I heard them pray, seen them give offering , then you begin to question yourself trying to make a clear distinction of what God said or they said; Confusion "I don't know everybody else seems to be OK with them.. "Well Maybe it's just Me"... No the devil is just a liar, No You are right on it, follow your gut feelings, if you are a praying holy ghost filled disciplined baptized clean living christian, "your antennas are not sending you false signals , pay close attention begin to watch with your spiritual eye listen with your spiritual ear.. Watch and pray and listen all at the same time, while their talking praying, singing, or whatever it is their doing, ask the Father to show you what spirit is at work here" each time your in their presence pray watch listen all at the same time; we can't go on fine sounding words If they will attempt to cast out demons when they KNOW" their just as wicked as the demon their attempting to cast out, their truly a master of deception; Demons know how to go hide.

Church Witches They hide behind their clothes, their Dress their vernacular even their smile, I believe demons control witches more than witches control demons. Witches do not necessarily look like witches they come in all shapes and sizes hair colors , bubbly young girls, athletic beauty queens, Teachers, House wife's, Nurses, Professional Women, the same is true for the Men. Many Women get into Witchcraft because of loneliness and unforgiveness in their heart; and they don't know Jesus; and it gives them some since of excitement like a game to play spying in on others and to laying snares , and conquering up evil spirits and sending them out to someone's house and then stand back watching and observing their targeted victim. Here are some Signs when Witchcraft is in operation..

Wanting to be alone

When we're confronted with a disturbing influence

Your sleep is disturbed

Fatigue and lack of energy to live day to day life

Fear for no reason

Wanting to be alone

Disinterest in life

feelings of hopelessness

Irritated for no reason

severe depression

dryness of mouth

Weight gain/Weight loss

Sudden Chills

Forgetful

Confusion

Crying

Dreams Blocked/Can't Remember

Objects can bring on attacks too, a demon may be assigned to a certain thing and will follow that object about.

Confusion Is a big one can't get thoughts together for love nor money everything is just off and scattered.

Witches steal the virtues of people and store them inside containers jars and throw the container into the sea, also peoples photographs are used they incite incantations over them and seal them up. I Pray In the Mighty name of Jesus Christ I take authority over anything concerning Me or My family that has been placed into any Water large or small for evil intent.. in the Mighty name of Jesus Christ I command the Sea and the land to cough it up" right now in Jesus name.

.Pad Locks are also used by Witches, this is a very imporantant tool used by Witch doctors & occultist they use Padlocks to lock up peoples destinies and other life things, Padlock Magic these enemies of God through the use witchcraft and Black Magic has used evil padlocks to tie up and lock down peoples destinies, marriages, finances, blessings, womb children, glory, unctions, mantles, ministries, and human progress. The padlock is a very important tool to Witchdoctors or anyone that Practices evil.. The only way you can open the padlock is to have the key in the spiritual realm keys is Revelation knowledge , sometimes they used more than one padlock; most of the time, more than one evil Padlock is used to lock up someones destiny ...7 Padlocks can be used at one time and you must unlock each one of them through prayer to get totally free. There was a entire family that an aunt had cursed all her sisters children .. the preacher ask how many children does your mother have? He replied 5 children sir" the Deliverance Minister told the young man that he must bring 5 Padlocks to represent each child. He would pray over them and open up and all the children s destinies would then be restored.. I read that the occultists calls the persons name so many times over the open padlock and say whatever they want to be locked... Father God "you know the person reading this right now.. If their life has been frustrated through evil padlock.. Father I command every evil Padlock no matter how many, all of them to be open today! and I command everything to be untied and restored that has been held up due to their evil undetermined efforts.. Their Glory, Their Honor, Their Success Their Influence, Their Health... BE RESTORED in the Mighty Name Of Jesus the Christ.

Your Information is the key that the enemy is feeding on to bewitch you, In the kingdom of darkness information is vital, they use your information to take you Captive, Social Media Sites where people put all their business and post all their pictures and things that made them smile, evil workers just love this! Many people are taking this for granted because they just want to be popular.. It's a low down shame, that some people's hearts are black as dirt and they would rather see someone sad and hurt, rather than smiling and happy with joy... "Because lawlessness is increased, most people's love will grow cold...Matthew 24:12.ASB

Just as we Prepare for rain by carrying along our umbrella we must prepare for the agents of Satan just the same preparing by learning his tactics, 2 Corinthians 2:11 Says so we won't be outwitted by Satan. It hard for someone to trick you when your knowledgeable of their schemes".. Accepting their friend request gives them permission to see and even to astral project into your bedrooms at night and other places, they can see you and begin to monitor you.. Satan has agents" they take your picture, copy and paste it into their shrines, or print copies for their evil altars.. And the person (the victim) has no clue, that their sitting right beside the very person every single day at their workplace that's causing all the trouble.

This book is not to frighten but just to make one aware of things, Boxers watch and study videos of their opponent all the time..Why? To see how he fights, going into the ring, It would be foolish of me not to try and get as much information on my opponent as I can" to help me win the fight and to stand against him.. study his moves, his techniques, his approach. I once jokingly stated that I can picture Satan in the Mirror full of young boy pride popping his collar saying "yeah let me see how many of these Fools I can get today"

But if we're walking in the wisdom of the holy spirit, folly and destruction will have a very hard time overcoming us.. Ask the spirit of wisdom to fill you with discernment to make you sharp, Wisdom gives the ability to discern good from evil, right from wrong, angels from demons, and the wise from the foolish. Wisdom discerns evil and hates wickedness, when we have the Holy Spirits Wisdom we can see God's perspective and truth for our lives. No one can just tell you anything. If you get something outside of God's will, you'll have to stay outside of his will to keep it,

We are truly living in the last day's as we read the Holy scriptures and watch the daily news or just simply take a look around, The bible is fulfilling itself everyday, and we've got to be aware of our surroundings and move with a military mind" the mind of a solider because truly we are in a war and deception abounds.. Satan's Servants disguise themselves as angels of light they are deceitful workmen

For there shall arise false Christs, and false prophets, and shall shew great signs and wonders; insomuch that, if it were possible, they shall deceive the very elect. Matthew 24:24 KjV

False Christ... Shall arise, of course along with false Prophets but the false Christ stands out loud to me I've pondered somewhat on this thing, their performing signs and wonders... people are creating things and saying it's Christ Jesus, The Christ but it's not! You ever get those little stickers post on your social media page or text saying something about Jesus pass this on to fifteen people and you'll get a blessing" I got one recently... here's a hug it read" with a the person doing the hugging made out of newspaper, shortly after receiving it I began to feel a bit confused and strange I was driving when I received it, when

I stopped to get gas "I noticed that my good alright feeling had change to a low degree, I ask the Holy Spirit what was wrong what is it God..?

My Phone came to mind, I got back into the car and checked it" Had your hug today'? Caught my attention so now, If I receive anything they are Instantly erased. This is Demonically Ordained from it's originator it's creator it's founder.. It's a false Christ It has satanic ties attached to it to burden you, with false burdens and I see people just forwarding them, It's a demonically linked accursed chain to get to all the Christians, people In general Satan will ensnare anybody available, and now the accursed thing is riding with you everywhere you go.

Demonic Portals are extraordinary openings in space or time that connects in this case, evil travelers to distant realms and are created by evil workers so that demons,and demonic entities can use to travel to and from distant realms, it can be a shortcut it's a doorway or a gateway a large entrance, or exit opening..It provides access or links to other sites; like a tunnel ..There can also be hidden portals that you can't see.

Portals can also be opened on telephone lines and cell phones for eaves dropping. A clicking sound will be heard as if another receiver has been picked up in another room and it will sound as if you're talking into a wide opening, space tunnel your voice is being pulled into a hole.. A portal has opening up. The thing to do is for both parties to disconnect the call on the count of three, And Or Before your call is Made pray against eaves dropping spirits, command all portals and leylines to be closed and frozen tight, ask for the assistance of angels to be posted at all four corners of the call to block any demonic activities and take authority over the airways in Jesus Name.

Satanic Agents are called by a code, a code that is given to them at the time of their joining along with blood devil worshipers have to live off the blood of humans Isaiah Chapter 66..Kjv

This code MUST be cast out of the body of the satanic agent and their blood some satanic agents, their code is carried in their blood If the code is not cast out during Deliverance the Satanic Agent has not been delivered the Demons can still make contact with the agent.. And the Agents Know This"

Blood suckers suck blood from people in the spiritual realm and the unsuspecting victims will began to feel weak and tired and a little depressed as this evil deed is being done, the children of darkness they do this just by standing next to the person I read that they scan the person first, to make sure that their not a Christian, because if the person is a christian and they take in their blood, they would become very sick.. Glory Halleluiah!

These Agents are sitting up strong in the churches (Isaiah 14:13.) Kjv

I Myself have encountered Many of these Children of Darkness in disguised for some reason they always knew Me and I knew them.. The next thing I knew the person would be trying to secretly remove Me for Fear that I would expose them; a time or two it has been the Pastor's Wife.

When they have an assignment they come in and sit at the back of the church and study the Pastor, and everything going on inside the church, and who is who; study his weakness because after all He or She is still only human. It could be a weakness for Chocolate Cake, They'll work with that" for starters.

They ware bands and spiritual rings that are not seen with the naked eye, Upon entering the Church they take these evil rings and throw them in front of the church each ring will have a evil spirit attached to it, one could be labeled lust to release lust spirits in the church among the members the other could be Sickness, Unhappiness and so on . There are two types arm rings are one and finger rings. They want to collect the churches harvest the souls that are coming in.

Children' Of darkness connect with these spirits through dance, singing, drums and the use of snakes which are called voodoo Serpents which they believe represents healing and knowledge and the connection between heaven and earth. Their main focus today is to influence the outcome of the life events of others. True rituals are done behind closed doors summoning demons Killing animals for sacrifices, drinking blood and eating abominable things.

One way that Satan Satanic agents can be identified Is by the waring of the ankle bracelet on the left ankle, the left foot has a toe ring, also the left side nostril a ring; They focus totally on the lift side. They give false hope as the angel of light pump up others by telling the person to be more cockey, and to take charge of their life's they come off as if everything is always alright at all times in their lives they seem to have everything that the other person does not have, They'll give the person whatever they are in need of their not giving out of love or care for the person truth is they don't care about you" ! their giving is to get closer to winning their target over, and to Make their master Satan proud; and to gain more power in the demonic ranking realm and their goal is to try to get the person to become like them acting prideful with an attitude displaying that their the best at everything they set their precious hands to . Christ's character is not prideful or cockey.

The devil is so good at cunning and craftiness he can disguise anything and make a religious capital out of it. And have such a one thinking that the evil that they are doing is justified with God. This is one of Satan's specialties to hide under christian disguise's at the same time. There are people who practice bible reading and the occult at the same time and teach Sunday School play with occult Magic Boards and will stand up" and prophesy and act as if Jesus Christ himself gave them the divine revelation information... (The Devil Is a Big Fat Lie) To mistake gifts that come about from the kingdom of darkness to be holy.

Spiritual Deception is at an all time high, so many impostors among us, evil deceivers wolfs in sheep's clothing.

...Matthew 21..Not everyone who says to Me, 'Lord, Lord,' will enter the kingdom of heaven, but only he who does the will of My Father in heaven.

I believe in these last days the main two spirits that will rule in the end against the body of Christ are Jezebel and Delilah... Remembering Jezebel

Jezebel was a Phoenician princess in the 9th century who married **Ahab**, the prince of Israel. Eventually, they ruled as king and queen. Jezebel continued worship the **nature god Baal**. Her citizens and the **Yahweh** prophet **Elijah** despised such actions. Jezebel persecuted the prophets

of Yahweh, and fabricated evidence of blasphemy against an innocent landowner who refused to sell his property to King Ahab, causing the landowner to be put to death. For these transgressions against God and the people of Israel, Jezebel met a gruesome death—thrown out of a window by members of her own court retinue, and the flesh of her corpse eaten by stray dogs.

In the biblical story, Jezebel became associated with false prophets. In some interpretations, her dressing in finery and putting on makeup[3] led to the association of the use of cosmetics with "painted women" or prostitutes.

More reading about Jezebel can be found in the book of 1kings Chapter 16

The Spirit and the characteristics that describes this Woman can not to be taken lightly..LEVIATHAN THE SEA MONSTER. Isaiah 27:1* Job 41

Is a whale with tremendous strength, described as powerful and dangerous, Job 41:8 say's.. "if you lay a hand on It, You will never forget the battles that follows. NLT.

Through Research I found that this spirit is also joined closely with the Jezebel spirit, and It's aim is to afflict those that are anointed for the kingdom of God.

....................ADD LEVIATHAN HERE...................

Devious in nature, hates authorities unless its to gain favor to help accomplish his or her agenda.

This spirit has the ability to love and hate at the same time, She kills the anointing of the person because once the anointing is gone, the person has nothing left to fight with, So if he or she is successful is the process of stripping one of their anointing then she has the rest of you. The Jezebel Spirit has 21 personalities. This spirit gives an appearance of sorrowful repentance and then it will attack, They need to be praised and get others to praise them.. they have possessive love, their love is controlling, they're alright until you disagree with them always in rebellion against leadership. The person with this spirit will never admit their wrong unless it gains them favor. This is a very cunning and seductive spirit it is the most active spirit at work INSIDE the church today.

She or He is quick to spritutualizes Everything when confronted explaining it off on God, this prevents him or her from owning up to responsibility.

They like to be the center of attention, doesn't like to see others recognized.

Will quickly undermine another accomplishments

Pushy and domineering they make others think they don't have enough sense to think for themselves.

They enjoy using the element of surprise, loves to catch someone off guard like showing up a day early for a Meeting,

Will tell half truths.

Will stop at nothing to destroy someone's reputation.

Star Marine Kingdom:

As I stated earlier that this Kingdom has many components and Marine always Means Water, they are strong and stubborn spirits very evil and demonic, Anything that has to do with water is mostly of a female gender. There is a connection between the waters and whoredom; sexual looseness in riverine areas.

In the Marine Kingdom Stars have and hold an important meaning, Stars are their way of showing that they are in control and have authority over an an area.. nothing wrong with the star itself, but its what evil workers do with it. Its been said that by deliverance Ministers of today that its not an easy tast to deliver a person who is under the influence of these type spirits, as stated before they are very stubborn and difficult to deal with. The victims of these demons have stars on their foreheads these are high ranking demons.. And I'm not glorying them in any way" JESUS CHRIST IS Lord Over All.. However its My assignment to report all Information to the body of Christ so we can War effectively even the more , After all We're going to defeat the works of the enemy, not be defeated by the the works of the enemy. We won't be destroyed for a lack knowledge.. In Jesus Name Amen.

These are high ranking demons, high ranking cults.. Masons 3rd degree

when these spirits are present they make one bold in the mouth when speaking glamorous and seductive in speech, they pump one to talk.

There is such a thing called Marine Sickness, A sickness that Doctor's cannot diagnose in the natural.

* Marine virgin means the demons have forbided the person to Marry, the Woman will have a star on the inside of their Private Parts, If that star is not broken the Man will suffer much loss and could even die. If a person Marries anyway their spouse will suffer Marine Percussion because the star means virginity, The Private parts of that Woman has been marked and dedicated to those demons.

If the Star is on the outside of the body" they can Marry, but the children will be jacked up and problematic...Break the birthmark of the Marine Kingdom. Marine demons are very wicked, People who know about them say, one can be possessed by them" just by touch.. If your life pleases God he will take care of you.

Marine Jezebel this one pollutes Men sexually out to destroy mankind. When a Man has sexual intercourse with one of these Spirits after-wards the person becomes uncontrollable and craves Sex like food or a baby craves warm milk in a bottle and begins to loose everything of value it becomes swallowed up by the water kingdom. There is the celibate Marine Marine witchcraft,Tree Marine,Lake Marine, Vampire Marine.

Water Dog Spirit (Pepta) Philippians 3:1-2 Revelations 22:15

Watch Them Dogs! Beware of evil workers they're conning and sly. The famous sermon comes to mind that the late grate B.W Smith SR. Preached.. ( Watch Them Dogs.) Which is available on you tube.

Dreadlocks's are believed to be of the Marine Spirit's kingdom

The Women that have their hair in dreadlocks's are bound to the waters of the marine kingdom, while doing research for this book I came across one lady that describe an experience she had, who is not a christian but believes that there is a creator, she strikes Me as one who has life figured out by way of science; the earth and the Moon gods. She spoke of receiving information from her ancestral heritage and the use of crystals. She recalled a dream that she had , she stated that she was planing to cut her loc's off and return to regular black hair styles.. and in a dream someone came to her and told her not to cut them.. she went on to say that when she first locked her hair, How she felt a magical shift in her soul, as she put it" and awoken her spirituality within; She stated, that her senses opened up even the more, and she described how she felt a supernatural drawing towards the ocean, which was something that she already loved and adored .. The Water; The Beach,The Ocean.. It called for her to come, She felt that this was a good thing how she had spirituality connected with the waters.

Groves and Trees.

**Exodus 34:13 KJV**

But ye shall destroy their altars, break their images, and **cut down their groves**:

A **sacred grove** or **sacred woods** or any grove of trees that are of special religious importance to a particular culture. Sacred groves feature in various cultures throughout the world. They were important features of the mythological It's believed that trees have a sacred wisdom... Isa 1:29 for you shall be ashamed of the oak trees in which you take pleasure and you shall blush

There is nothing wrong with trees itself or planting a tree, which is a beautiful thing to do, However some people have found trees to be used for more than just shelter and shade and memories.

Trees and forests provide a habitat for many species of animals and plants. Tropical rainforests are among the most biodiverse habitats in the world. Trees provide shade and shelter, timber for construction, fuel for **cooking** and heating, and fruit for food, as well as cold winter nights at home by the fireplace.

I have found that trees are heavily used in occultists rituals, and I'm here to expose it and open blind eyes, Such as mine were..

I always share the story about the tree leaves that were placed in front of the door of home, And I know it was Jesus that alerted me of the scheme, Now I aware that the wind blows leaves, but these leaves were not scattered throughout the lawn just around the entrance of the door area, and there was no tree in my yard that matched those exact leaves. That's when My eyes became open. "Hmmm... It must be something to theses trees' and I found out that it sure is, just as is with the chicken and its eggs,the parts of the fowl are used in many occult rituals that take place under trees

The children gather wood, and the fathers kindle the fire, and the women knead

their dough, to make cakes to the queen of heaven, and to pour out drink offerings

unto other gods, that they may provoke me to anger. Jeremiah 7:18..KJV

The Queen of heaven was the fertility goddess, Ashtoreth, Astarte or Ishtar), worshiped

in Assyria and Babylon. Her worship involved sexual immorality, And provoked God to God to anger.

Occultists,Witches, They use trees to carve images

**Isaiah 44:19 King James Version (KJV)**

19 And none considereth in his heart, neither is there knowledge nor understanding to say, I have burned part of it in the fire; yea, also I have baked bread upon the coals thereof; I have roasted flesh, and eaten it: and shall I make the residue thereof an abomination? shall I fall down to the stock of a tree?

**Isaiah 44:20 King James Version (KJV)**

20 He feedeth on ashes: a deceived heart hath turned him aside, that he cannot deliver his soul, nor say, Is there not a lie in my right hand?

These scriptures are talking about trees that have been used in witchcraft, and occult magic, they plant things under them, pray to them.. I read one book, that said if your feeling some kind of way, if you sit under a certain type of tree, The tree will soak up the blues and feelings of melancholy. Each tree has a supernatural meaning that the practitioner is looking for in order to produce a certain type of effect that they are trying to achieve in order to get the wanted outcome. This is refereed to as plant wisdom.

Let;s go deeper in the occult and expose more of Satan's evil secretes and devices

Candles are found to be very important to evil workers, Candles became more popular and useful when the the evil workers started hiding their secret science work behind closed doors, Taking down the signs and everything was brought down to a whisper And when they shall say unto you, Seek unto them that have familiar spirits, and unto wizards that peep, and that mutter: should not a people seek unto their God? for the living to the dead?

… as their families began to grow and have children and grandchildren and so forth.. The evil family business" became an embarrassment at school and for the children and places of work, finding employment making friends dating, and was just a stigma on the entire family line.

So when I pray I sure don't forget about the the ones burning candles for my demise they have colors for this spell and that curse on this certain day's and sugar or Karo syrup is used if they want a sweet outcome the candle is burned sitting in sugar or Karo syrup or some type sweetener to sweetening the outcome..ie

There was a woman that couldn't pay her rent for 6 Months and would burn satanic candles sitting them in some type of sweetener on behalf of her landlord to keep from being evicted this techniques she believed would hold off the land landlord until she got the money to pay the back rent.. this evil deed is also practiced by landlords also to remove unwanted tenants. Some say that they burn candles to bring peace, or to bring back a lover that has left or vice Versa to send one away. "For Money to come to them, even call for someone elses Money to come to them, or to curse a relationship, They burn to cursed money also and give it to their victim, whom the evil worker dislikes and has an evil agenda against, and wishes to curse and destroy their finances etc.. In the name of Jesus Yashua I blow out! every satanic candle burning against me,Any evil money spent on my behalf to curses my finances, My income as a whole, my marriage, my destiny, in the mighty name of Jesus I rebuke over throw cast down, in Jesus name and replace with well wishes, In the mighty name of of Jesus.. Amen

Points Of Contacts.

Evil workers take pride in having something of theirs in their victims possession which could be a simple gift given at Christmas time, or a birthday present,or a simple (just because); As long as they have a point of contact, they have a way of getting on the inside through satanic focus and concentration A Point Of Contact is a tangible object that has been demonically charged with evil, and then given as a gift to a person. It could be something that has been intentionally left behind by someone on purpose, there has been times I have gotten in My car and went behind a visitor that has left my home.. and said " hay you left this".. Points of contact could be a person that is in the house or on the Job etc. fake friendships on assignment... An evil worker might say something like.. " I need a point of contact so I can get information on my target, I always beware when someone starts asking a lot of questions my antennas automatically go up.

Points Of contact.. once made aware of there assistance if at all possible they need to be removed and destroyed, Remember how the children of Israel could not stand before their enemies until the Acurseth thing was removed.. joshua7:13.

Also in the book of Acts.. Evil workers brought their books and burn them before all Men.. acts 19:19

Occult paraphernalia often serves as a seal to demonic attacks, they establish a point between you and the hostile forces they set up entrapment's so they can easily establish a forced entry. A tattoo can be an evil point of contact for demons, an evil mark.

When a person go's to see a psychic or palm reader or a medium root worker any of these type people, this is also is a point of contact to everybody in your family including little nieces and little nephews and little cousins too, whom have absolutely no knowledge of anything evil or demonic little joey is just learning to ride his bike or even tie his or her shoes. While your little niece just got her learners permit to drive, but a covenant has been made with the kingdom of darkness because perhaps the oldest brother on her father side which would be her first cousin has gotten into some trouble with the law, and daddy's brother uncle Nick has taken him to see somebody to help get him our of the trouble. You would think that has nothing to do with my household.. but it's in the family line now, the door has been opened to that family line.. And God forbid that uncle Nick needed to borrow $200 from someone in the family before he went. Where has your name or my name been taken too? In the name of Jesus Christ any Power calling my name or my family members name for evil die right now in Jesus name.

Evil workers, and when I say evil workers I mean all of them who are representing the kingdom of darkness, Warlocks the voodoo priest, satanist, shamans, root workers, Witches and the alike.. They are so evil these people do things like place their sickness and pain on others.. In the name of Jesus Christ You will not carry anybody elses load.

Let me tell you something" Many people will move away to another state or town trying to get away from the evil they are experiencing and go to some other place and find the same thing taking place" I want to shed some light here;

In the demonic kingdom just like in the kingdom of God when we first get saved "you know how bible say's the angels rejoice well the same go's in the the kingdom of darkness the rejoice also.. and remember I was telling you about the bell that go's off in the spiritual realm announcing their arrival into the demonic kingdom. So all over the world evil workers hold a certain place, well when the kingdom of darkness has a hit out for someone or someone from the evil kingdom its like a Load Board.. The assignment is placeded on that Load Board and where ever you relocate too, the evil workers in that land will pick it up and when they go to their Load Board.. their Satanic (ALTERS).. aka Load Board)..they will see the assignment awaiting .. They will see the hit out for You.. That's why I always Stress to You come against their evil alters silence them. Remember they are hungry for power and in the demonic kingdom, they respect POWER Not Titles, but Power" and any so called take down' they can achieve large or small begets the satanic agent more points more power; So now" you know you know how the scripture 1 Thessalonians 5:12 know them that labor among you, Know their Nature, Its two sides to this.. Know them to recognize them with respect, because they are over you in the Lord. And if their wicked you should be knowledgeable of that as well.. And not just leadership but all that labor among you. Draw near unto Me and I will tell you things that you did not know..Jeremiah 3:33

Ask and you shall receive.. Hevenly Father did you send this person into My life? Hevenly Father what is their purpose in My life? If it's an evil one" Father reveal all who's involved and why. And it's OK to asked God why, Jesus asked on the cross Father Why have thou forsaken me..Matthew 27:46

So we wonder why is the same thing happening in this Marriage, at this Job. In this new town this new house. In the Name Of Jesus I release blindness and confusion on every evil observer monitoring Me, I destroy all eyes of darkness assigned against Me watching Me Monitoring Me.. Evil Tracers trying to locate My whereabouts..Rebuke their evil pursuing Powers and Scatter them In Jesus Name Amen.

Demonic & Satanic Tools.

Altho I' don't believe I could ever know all the ends and outs about this subject/ slash/ topic demonic tools .."there are many things that can be used and made into a evil demonic tool when I say' anything, "I do mean anything, any item, an evil spirit can be called into an object and then that object placed into someones home office or church as a guardian angel so to speak" they believe, or fashioned to bring harm or misfortune; however a demon can live inside or be placed upon an object for a temporary time frame or permanent or even worn on the body, placed in the hair, or under someones skin.. but in this case I'm speaking of the object placed down inside the home office etc could be given as a gift, this makes it super easy for the person that gave the gift with the evil attachment to contact the spirit and give it instructions and make offerings to it; On the other hand the owner of the object may themselves had the evil placed believing that it will be protection of some sort for them.

A Demonic tool can be their evil wisdom giving them the satanic breakthroughs

Let's take a look at some other things used as tools and evil devices and also accessories

We discussed some things earlier concerning tools used on evil alters but here are some others to add to the long list.

Pins,nails, equal arm cross, cardinal points, pentagrams, hexagrams, incense, nets, scanners, demonic parties, blood covenants, covenants with the sun, moon, and stars, demonized money, candles, anything carved into an idol (wood), books, their area of expertize, water, perfumes, recipes, knifes, sacrificed animals, burnings, throwing of bones, cauldrons, washings, baths, chantings, knots& cords grindings, (graveyard items dirt stones flowers etc). black hens chickens, veils, demonic check points in the spirit realm, psychic gifts witches latter bird feathers, string of 9 knots, death spells , invoker of demons, marriages seduced by witchcraft,all devilish practices,false impressions, spiritual Marriage, occult covenants& sacrifices

All these things and more are used in their evil doings and the do have an effect on humanity.

Evil Sacrifices

Sacrifices are big business for evil workers all those who work demonic alters, their alters call for a sacrifice ,sacrifices are the voice of every alter, without a sacrifice their alter has no voice and cannot speak; the evil sacrifice and the evil exchange I'd say they work together and go hand in hand. The alter is the place where the sacrifice is taken then the priest invokes the deity, the evil alter is a gateway for evil spirits to go back and forth .If the alter is satanic then of course demons are present If the alter is of our God then Jesus is present. Remember Balak in numbers 22:24was so determined to curse Israel he built 21 alters to no avail.

Evil alters can be set up at the drop of a hat, here are some of the places where the evil sacrifices are taking place

At Crossroads, clothes, rivers and seas, woods, forest, on the body people literately become a walking alter for Satan. A family alter, waste dumping site spiritually the person will stink like the stench of the dumping place.

God will put people around you, And so will Satan, so therefore we must make an effort to know which ones is which," test them, investigate pray ask God to reveal to you who is for you and who is not for you-you want to make sure youre not eating and drinking with a judas, Who will sale you to the highest bidder without the slightest thought .Make every to show love and goodwill to all Men but the truth is many people today are beyond disloyal, self centred even Jesus knew his enemy how much more should we?" Deception Abounds, Wolves in sheep clothing are everywhere and are hard at work against us we must have on the full armor of God and be sober minded and alert, for our enemy is on the prowling around seeking whom he may devour 1Peter 5:8

**We must seek God's face, least we play right into the plan of the enemy.**

For one to assume that they have no enemies and that everybody likes and loves them is just plain stupid and not a good position for one to take. I had a co worker once tell me.." Tammy you love everybody, But everybody don't like and love you."

Prayerfully Investigate and God will give you the plans and details of their agenda against you, He will show you their heart no matter what their mouth is saying they pretend to be saved to gain creditability with people and the church.. Isaiah 8:19...Say's My People Can

Require Of Me. We don't have to consult mediums or spirits the dead on behalf of the living for life's answers "We God's Children can go to our Heavenly Father our God is alive and well and eagerly awaiting us to come unto him.

Jeremiah 33:3.. "I will tell you great and mighty things that you did not Know." Prayer is your only hope of Identifying Satan's agents that have been planted around you. People are sold out to the service of Satan, As you remember 911 his agents are willing to lay down their lives for their king Lucifer.

---

They corlate with the phases of the moon.

Isa 57:8 behind bedroom doors you have put your pagan symbols zach12:2lay siege against us God will make us a very heavy stone unto them, strike every horse and its rider with blindness and confusion and madness.

---

Satan will not sit quietly by and let us achieve all our goals, or allow anything to go according as planned, So we can have a reason to give praises to God, He definitely wants to bring all our praises to God to a screeching halt, Stop him before he stops you. Don't just allow the enemy to just have at;" and run loose in your life, He will try to create situations to make us think that even the Holy Bible is a lie, that Jesus Christ doesn't love us, let alone care anything for us, take these thoughts captive and cast them quickly out of your mind. He wants you to second guess everything you know is true; So Therefore do everything you can to stay spiritually connected, and covered, with back up Give pay a tithe, Study his word, stay in the fold fellowshipping with the brethren. I know one of the enemies tactics is trying to get us away from the fold out by ourselves so he can tell us lies about the Church, Its members, The Pastor, Family, and Friends, He just want us to loose out in every area, that way he can say " see there's no God" If it was why are you so downtrodden, why are you sick? Why is it so much suffering in the world? Because of him!" (Satan) The father of lies.

God Is For Us.

- ~ Satan Cannot stand resistance.
- ~ Satan loves to debate and argue until it turns violate.
- ~ Satan absolutely Cannot stand the blood of Jesus Christ.
- ~ Satan ensnares and entraps through thrill seeking curiosity and excitement. Curiosity kill the cat.

Satan is a constant aggressor and bombards us Everyday with lies and half truths trying to make one think that they have not been forgiven of their sins; He loves to see us confused and in condemnation he attacks the mind. We must be super quick to cast them all down because if you don't the battle is lost, You and I must keep up the shield of faith and not replay old things over and over.. fret not thyself because of evil doers, Satan is definitely the most evil doer that there is.

He and his demonic crew mostly loves to attack the nation changers the three spirits that work closely with him is the

- Spirit of Jezebel
- The spirit of death and hell
- Spirit of the anti-christ

These are generals under him, His main counter parts

He loves when people deny his existence, He binds the strong man and then plunders his house...Mark 3:27 No one enter into a strong mans house and steal his goods unless he first bind/tie the owner of that house up and then he can plunder his goods.. Matthew 12:29.. Evil workers can do binding spells to make a person not want to- want to do anything or say anything, just be in a slump not want to pray or seek the Lord or read their Bible, Not even want to speak up and talk for themselves their so called binding spell takes away ones effort to fight and their get up to do something, Then one can easily be plundered without difficulty.

The book of Isaiah say's ...Loose Thyself it is a powerful verse that relates to self deliverance Isaiah 52:2..NKJV We have been given the power and authority to loose ourselves from all types of bondage; To put a stop to whatever the enemy is trying to do.

Matthew 16:19 I give you the keys to the kingdom of heaven and whatever you bind on earth will be bound in heaven and whatever you loose on earth will be loosed in heaven. NKJV

Basically the kingdom of heaven has your back, it will back you up in all your endeavors. I'm thinking about the kingdom keys, They will allow a deeper revelation than just what's on the surface to open up to you even the more, Jeremiah 3:3 Says.. Call unto me and I will answer you, and show you great and mighty things which you do not know. NKJV. It is so much more I feel to be said concerning kingdom keys- Keys are not just given to anyone God has to be able to trust you with the revelations you receive and the kingdom secrets, People who act foolishly loud and proud, immature and unstable ordinarily don't get to hold keys. God's kingdom is to be entered with a Holy reverence and respect and thankfulness; the keys represent authority for entry. God delegated his authority by way of the keys.. Delegated- To entrust a task or responsibility to another person.

**Keys represent Authority for entry.**

**Demons.**

Anything related to Satan's kingdom will attract demons, sinful activities going on We must be on guard about what comes into our home least you be ensnared by it. Deut 7:25-26

Demons are definitely attracted to houses by objects and also literature that pertain to false religions, occult books, cults, if you are having problems with demons disturbances it could very well be to some objects in your home with occultic ties to them or a gift that was given or clothing or a piece of furniture, antiques that you've collected or inherited, yard sales and goodwill items, be on the look out for this sort of thing, Who knows the pretty little pink lamp you purchased to go with that new bed spread used to belong to a Daughter of Satan a Witch.

This brings me to the lie Christian Witch, "What in the world" Where did this crazy term come from? There is no such thing as a Christian Witch

God said in exodus 22:18 KJV.. Thou shall not suffer a witch to live; Witchcraft is no game, God would have all witches exterminated, Their wickedness is so great before him until he said that they should not even be aloud to live, The spirit of God does not live in a witch. The word Christian is a representation of Christ Jesus Christ. I know the enemy is fighting me right here, Because I'm getting tired and it's becoming a challenge to keep focus, But right here I'm about to go in deep and look at their curse's and characteristics and their secrets I'm about to put them on blast" as these kids say.

" I have a saying, I don't care about anyone being a witch if you are an adult and you so choose to be a witch" hay do your thang, but please know that you are going to hell if you don't change.. The bible clearly say's that those who do this sort of thing won't enter the kingdom of heaven Galatians 5:19-21. Acts of the flesh, sexual immorality, impurity and debauchery, drunkenness orgies, fits of rage, orgies and last but not least WITCHCREAFT, Those who live like this will not inherit the kingdom of God.

If you have any good looks about you, know that a witch will try to steal your beauty, Yes they want to see you ugly and unpleasant in your appearance, She will have an evil eye on you to steal your beauty. During the times their up to their workings against you can look under their eyes and see darkness rims and circles more than usually if you know them. This priceless info came from one of Gods precious gem in the Lord at Praise Report Ministries Apostle A Lavonne amen thank you for that. A witch always wants to give you something, discussed earlier as a point of contact, and they will want something from you, something with your DNA sent body odor and there are some curses that they do that requires something to be stolen from their victim; Something that has been worn and not washed, they must have something of their targeted persons in their possession. I'm here to tell you they are so slick in their ways, the things I've witness that (they) witches will do, to try to retain something of yours or from your home or to get something in your home; I have found phone books on my porch, when at&t had not sent out any new phone books, flyers left on my car at the local Walmart, be careful what you find outside the door of your house flyers and business cards etc anything they can get you or I to bring inside ours homes it will have a demonic charge on it and cause you problems and once again be used as a point of contact against you and your family . Witches are very cleaver always thinking of ways to trap us and ensare us that's why we must be sharp with decernment. They are Married to the devil, They want to be near the true saints of God and trust me, they do know who the true saints of God are, So that they can memic us because they" just like their father the devil they cant produce anything, They can know the words of the bible but they cannot amply inturpit it because the holy spirit dose not live in a witch and never will. The Python spirit resides in witches the spirit of the snake this is a witchcraft spirit all day long. These witches pretend to be saved only to gain creditbility with the church and any time she or he sings in the service they are puluting the service. Locator amulets charms they use to locate people's where a bouts; Charms are everything to them theye're always looking for intergredents to make a charm, It's like there's an app for that. Backwardness they do things in a reverse or upside down like upside crosses, any holy thing they will do it in a backwards way like the holy communion instead of drinking it as if drinking water they will place it under their tounge and not over, drinking blood and eating flesh Isaiah 66:17..

Some are not a part of a coven but solitude. Earth Magic located to finding auras at long distances, ley line magic, is that earth magic as well; sympathetic magic is used to influence a person and or things that have once been in contact with each other and continue to act on each other at a distance after the physical contact has been severed.

Another thing vitally important to these evil workers are the Orishas which are the seven African Powers.. The Orishas give these workers of iniquity answers to do their spells, they are demi gods, they are their messengers they are recognized by their different colors and markings and numbers they are spirit guides they believe that the orishas rule over the forces of nature and the endeavors of humanity, Santeria and Yoruba deities they are believed to be powerful but mortal spirits. An Orisha is a manifestation of Olodumare a (god) I don't even want to give them the respect of the use of a Capital letter in this book. I can't believe how these people can see this as factual and true realistic God in their lives. "But Ok, Deep Breath Moving right along. Glory be to the Lord Jesus Christ He has allowed me to expose them they are 7 names that I came across in my studies there could be more, You are now ready to begin your own research and continue learning how to defeat and bring down another one of Satan's tools against us. (The Orishas) Silence and rebuke their powers In Jesus Name rebuke their lunar schedule, the way they do things according to the timing and phases of the moon, their feast days when they make food sacrifices to theses demi gods each one had a pacific day I saw Sun through Mon, rebuke their cooking pots and cloths and knifes and also where there placed at in homes and offices I even saw that one of the demi gods can even be placed inside the library even had one that served the fireplace.

Green and black bracelets serve as a trademark too.

Rebuke their Alters too, One can even be small enough to fit inside a bag or pocket.

A good thing to keep in mind is that these people are devoted to their evil doings, It's no small game, They want to move up in the ranks and will do just about anything; When the Church Is Asleep. I read that after some Inishations the canidate is requied to ware white for seven day's.

ASTRAL PROJECTION/OCCULT TRAVELLER

The Heavenly father has blessed me with more information on this subject this matter fuels my holy anger like no other, For someone to be able to secretly be in your house/bedroom watching you, watching you undress and or do the things you do in private it's beyond disturbing.. It has been my prayer for quite some time now, on how to dethrone these invaders I've heard it said that whatever you suffer through that's the area of your anointing; and power you'll have power over that particular thing'. "So If that's the case I've got this in the bag" and waring the tee shirt, These entities have been a disturbance in My Car, and in My Bedroom Doctors office Work place, I've been dealing with this way more than I care to talk about, My husband not so much, He says not for him he always felt that if someone wanted to watch him in that Manor" Their the one's with the problem Not Me" he'd confidently say, with all his male swag working they need to get a life whomever they are.

They are Witches They need to give you something a (gift) or just anything in your home, office, work place, car to connect to you with to build a leyline and portal that way they can have a straight point of contact to travel straight through to their target. And know this also beware of giving out your telephone number or Who your giving it to give it to the right person and it could be like giving a key to your house, the enemy's kingdom uses numbers telephone numbers are tied to us through our name .. Cover all your numbers SSN too.

MONITORING SPIRITS

Rebuke every human Spirit & Spying spirit monitoring you, they hate you and I so much" That they will follow us around daily like Spy's they're not all knowing like Jesus Christ, They need to gather all the information they can to build a file and build a plan against Us , They wish to hinder our Way and our prayers any way they can, making sure that nothing good comes our way, These Ones like to give gifts too, They seek out a legal right to attack Us, There are folk in the flesh that the enemy has sent that will eat with you laugh with you and dance and all the time be hoping for your down fall those ones that are assigned against us on private missions. You'll find that something you've shared with them that you liked or that meant a little something to you anything personal , you'll return to it and learn that it's No longer there anymore, or the thing that made you the most happiest it's been suddenly changed or discontinued, or broken or just something to make you feel sad at heart in dis belief and this was only after you told them how much You liked a thing.

All astral vision and hearing be shut down and blinded by the finger of the almighty God in Jesus Name.

"Ok I get that, I'm a believer also, But for me it was not acceptable at all! Prophets are highly sensitive to the spiritual realm, the unseen is seen and also felt by them.

So needless to say much prayer and study has gone forth on this topic and also being viewed as mentally unbalanced at times yelling at the air "GET OUT OF HERE IN JESUS NAME! and your family looking with a ? mark Face" back and forth at you and then at what seems to be" to them thin air.. There's No one in here honey but you and I" Who are you talking too?"

So after years of going through this sort of thing he now knows that I'm not Coo Koo after all. Trying to prove that something is present to someone who cannot see it in the physical was and is not easy.. So I had to teach him how to listen and pay attention to the atmosphere and also the shifting in the room when a demon has entered the temperaure in the room will change too.

THE SILVER CORD..ECCLESIASTES 12: 6-7

Yes remember your creator now while you are young, Before the silver cord of life snaps, And the golden bowel is broken and the pitcher is broken at the fountain, and the wheel is broken at the cistern; and the dust returns to the earth as it was, and the spirit returns to God who gave it.

This is scripture and prayer

## PRAYER AGAINST OCCULT TRAVELLERS

I come in the resurrected power and name of the Lord Jesus Christ To whom I belong

I take Authority over the airways I bind and forbid any quiet thing or person moving between the poles of this house In Jesus name.

I command in the mighty name of Jesus Christ every Astral Body traveling toward My home to become an Astral Corpse and fall to the ground in the mighty name of Jesus Christ,

I cancel and rebuke and overthrow all their systems correspondences right now in the mighty name of Jesus I command them to fail.. short circuit an die out! I bring them down to the ground to be powerless and Ineffective. I command life choking thorns of fire to overtake all their 22 nd astral paths. I decree and declare they shall stray and loose their way every time, at every attempt to mount up aginist this house, In Jesus name, I rebuke your cabalist path that takes you from one sephira to another.

I command all their astral regions to catch fire, May their Way and their astral flight Be Ensnared and deceived 333 times over in separate ways as HE/ SHE mounts up in route to this house In the Mighty Name Of Jesus.

, I Overthrow their diagram lines leading to this location in the name of Jesus, I decree and declare in the name of Jesus Christ that He / She shall not comfortably settle in their astral body, I command that they fall out of your astral body never to fit again ..."I rebuke his/her cabalist.. ..he/she shall not be able to rise in this house,

This house is off limits to any Occult Traveler In the name of Jesus.. he/she shall not rise in route to this house, In Jesus name, This house is dedicated to the Lord Jesus Christ Yeshua Hamashiach and does not allow occult travels;

Pitfalls shall overtake every occult travler in route to this house at every turn, In Jesus name.

I decree and declare that their guidepost shall become a stiff post, In Jesus Name;

I command all his/her fuel and blood supply to receive drain damage right now in Jesus mighty name; I send confusion into their astral trance I command their astral trance to be continually and perpetually broken I rebuke their ray direct with blindness let shame sit upon their houses and faces in Jesus name;

I command their imaginary astral body of light to become cold frigid def and blind; in Jesus name

I overthrow the horse and the rider I Perpetually forbid any astral body of light or astral animal to pass through our gates or any solid object or glass connected to this house or around or anywhere near this house or anywhere I am. In Jesus name.

I command their astral plane to become a world wind of fire. In Jesus mighty name, They shall not extend beyond our walls; I command their portals to be permently closed leading to this house, Nothing shall be clear or vivid in their astral viewing concerning this house in the name of Jesus..

I send the holy ghost FIRE to their threshold plane in yesod the sphere of the moon, And I break and Cancel their every covenant with the Sun

Moon and Stars In Jesus Name; I Send the Holy Ghost All Consuming Fire to all their Connecting points Above between and beneath traveling within the space of atom the proton, and all its meters I bring you down to the ground in total confusion .. In Jesus Mighty Name

AMEN:

Tamaria McRae

WICKED DECEPTION/ FAKE CASTING OUT

2Thessalonians 2:9

The Workings Of Satan:

Satan and his demonic agents they want to appear as, doing the work of an angel of light, but the workings are the workings of Satan's all the activities are satanic and demonic,, And perverted and false and are not the true signs and wonders of the one true living God. I had many thoughts about this because, I just knew if and when I saw a Minister cast a demon out Of someone I knew this was a true man or woman of God, 'So I thought, Oh how wrong I was.. I can recall this apostle, woman preacher whom Me and My family had come to adore and trust and believe in, deeply concerning the faith; I saw her command demons, Just the complete package for the glory of God, Until one evening she astral projected into my home while I was washing the dinner dishes, one occurrence of many'' That cause me to go to the father concerning her ..Lord " I asked have I been blindsided? only for him to reveal to me that this woman is playing a game I will never forget it A roll he said.." to be exactly clear, He told me that she cannot stand me, I was beyond crushed and sat quietly in disbelief for three days replaying the things Over and over I watched her do pertaining to the sacraments and ordinances of ministry, The times I was at her

Church, Well when I returned to myself again I vowed to tell everyone that this woman was not a true woman of God! The Lord stop me from doing so, "He told me that her influence is to large, He instructed me to let him do it!"

Another thing I've come to learn about these false workers they will kill to protect their secret from getting out their reptutation will be tanted and looking at Acts 16:16 after Paul cast out the spirit of divanation he was thrown into jail and all hell broke loose in the town and Paul and Salus were hated by everyone near and far, "so needless to say the backlash that comes off exposing THIS spirit is tremendous, Not to menschen This is a merchandising spirit too, it promotes to gain it's always out for gain because when the spirit was cased out their money stopped and they Got Angry Mad!

(This KIND does not come out except By Prayer and Fasting)

Matthew 17:21

They will stoop to all sorts of things to keep one from attending church the work place they, will shun you away,

And cause others to dislike you as well for no fault of yours. You haven't even told anyone you only yourself only know, But their terrified that you might do so, After this information is made known to you, by whatever means, One must also take precaution because now you have an enemy that will lay snares in your path, they will try to get rid of you by any means necessary; You are a threat to them, and always will be because you know their private business

2 Corinthians 12:12 Truly the signs of an Apostle were wrought among you in all patience in signs, and wonders and mighty deeds. People go to the devil/kingdom of darkness looking for power he will give them

that power their looking for, but with a cost of more than someone can afford to pay, in the end these folk find themselves all bound up confused and in need of direction healing.

After becoming a part of the kingdom of darkness they are able to transform themselves into animals, and walk through walls, see clearly at distance further than the normal eye can see, collect ones footprints, stare with they're eyes to cast a spell put sickness into people's bodies taking it off themselves and others that come to them in search of a demonic healing they will place sickness onto an incent poor helpless animal to rid one of sickness; Because if you remember Satan has no power to heal but to move things around with no victory He just places, it somewhere or on someone else because if he did really" he would have no kingdom the evil minister is also a captive of Satan. If advanced enough they will also have the ability to Opening locks quietly without keys, by chanting, They steal the minds of brilliant children and put it into other children "oh yes! Pastor Pat Holliday spoke about this on Miracle Internet Radio ON Blog Talk Radio. (Seduction of Christianity)

1st Thess5:21..But examine everything carefully hold fast to that which is good.

I found out that the kingdom of darkness has time sensitive assignments that they want carried out on time or else the demonic agent will reap a lashing of backlash I hear that it is so not good either nothing that we can Imagine

And this evil kingdom- they refer to us as cattle, and set up things that are imitations of us.

All Glory be to the Lord Jesus Christ who has allowed me to go into this dark world and study this enemy of ours and not be Afraid, that I may bring back to the body of Christ so that we may know his evil devices all the more The more we know about our enemy the less power he has over us, He can't trip us up so easily and throw us off track.

Just like I was telling someone just a moment ago.." that I noticed As I was coming into My Apartment Building I noticed that there were about 15 all white in color cigarette butts short and long lined up behind the row of parked cars stuck and pressed tightly in the concreate blocksI don't know what to call it exactly but the devided concreate I knew this was a form of witchcraft to try and bind the people the owner of these cars or trouble their homes.. now you know. Anything can be used as a occult object pray incantations over the item or they will burn evil candles and bring it to their enemies home threw in their yard place by their car or drop the item into something of theirs and the evil power will manifest

Things I've found out about the Pastors that are really of the Synagogue Of Satan.. Revelation 2:9 They support the cause of Satan theyre are many of them more than you can know. I'm Not telling you to frighten you but to Make you aware and on guard like the solder you are.

These false Ministers are equipped with a demonic powers and supernatural abilities that they receive from the Water Kingdom to falsely heal the very sickness that they've satanically inflicted onto a person, and In doing so they'll become recognized as a healer in the kingdom of God within the church, I should say. They will use the name of (Jesus) if they have too, they will agree with you if you say" but will not confess him by themselves' you won't hear of it spoken often from their lips, These Imposters mainly stick to the term god. But as you know the holy spirit is not there they are not inspired by the spirit as they claim, But are against Christ and are of the same spirit and character as the Antichrist .. It's a Satanic fire that they're in agreement with therefore their working together on one accord with the evil spirits to fool and bewitch the people.

**1 John 4:1... Beloved do not believe every spirit but test the spirits to see weather they are from God, Many false Prophets have gone out into the world.**

John the apostle told us to test the sprits to see weather they be of God, I use to personally wonder about that, How do I test a spirit? " properly Lord"? what do you do?" 1st In John said to try the spirits.. Meaning to check out by God's pattern or standard that never changes in verse 2 it says every spirit that confesseth that Jesus Christ came in the flesh is of God. Well if you recall just a few words back, I was saying they never say Jesus, You'll always hear god, god this, god that, but never will you hear them say Jesus the Christ!

**Goat Like Saints.**

Jesus said in Matthew 25 that he will separate the sheep from the goats meaning that he will judge which people or things in a group are bad (imposters) and which ones are good.. More and More people are taking up with this thing called Baphomet the symbol of a satanic goat its portrayed as a half human half goat figure or a goat head it has also been called the goat of mendes , the black goat and also the judas goat, the English occult historian montague summers suggested it was a combination of two Greek words, baphe and metis, or absorption of knowledge.

This information was taken from the Encyclopedia Of Demons and Demonology By.. Rosemary Ellen Gully

I tied them together because I have come up on many occasions on my Christian journey so called Christians that were pretending to be saved and the holy spirit reviled that they were children of Baphomet, teenagers and young boys and girls women, Men gangs and so forth are sold out to this Demon.

And it being in the form of the goat, and Christ saying that he;d separate the sheep from the goat" The Lord knows just what's going on here. They come to the alter crying fake tears after a good sermon. They're really good at spiritual deception most times when they do come to join a ministry their on an assignment to bring down that church and destroy every marriage in sight some characteristics I've noticed they make a big deal about prayer, Please don't misunderstand me" Of course prayer is important especially corporate prayer in the house of God'... But these imposters they will be over the top with it, they cannot say that Jesus is their Lord and savior Master over their lives, they will agree with you, but if you put them on the spot and they can't somehow get around it They might in order to stay under cover ; but they cannot make the declaration on their own. first John $4^{th}$ chapter. They will make a lot of valid strong points because they also have a word of knowledge and a word of wisdom; They may even seem to be getting aggressive.. At times concerning whatever they're pushing for to see happen within the church, They Will push to have small groups within the church, they work hard to separate married couples within the church saying" Woman together, Men together'" at times this can be lots of fun, If for a one night only sort Of kind Of thing, but definitely not indefinitely husbands and wives need to remain together and hear the same things being said and grow together not apart; But these imposters are wanting to divide in order to sew tares among the wheat, they'll also want to get rid of the older stronger mature saints; Not to mention the prophets; Prophets" they don't even have to be saying anything or doing anything they could just be there standing by the wall and they will cause so much friction in the enemies camp; Prophets make witches very nervous and uneasy So they'll do something to try to remove the anointed one there's something to be on watch for if you know for sure that Sister/Brother So N So is a true Prophet watch how he/she is treated by certain ones pay att Listen out" Do you notice that certain person always trying to get rid of Brother Michael (God's Prophet) on the sly'' nicely? Ahh" Brother Michael I saw a seat at another table over there.. I" mean it was more men on that side of the room.. I mean I'm just saying, Not trying to ger rid of you or nothing'' Just in case you didint want to sit on this side, slight laugh, centered around their sly words, trying now to clean it Up." You could also watch their body language, Facial expressions, Eyes when Brother Michael comes around, This could be Man or Woman the Jezebel Spirit absolutely hates the Prophet Of God.

**Ezekiel 34:17 And as for you, Oh My flock thus says the Lord God; Behold I judge between cattle and cattle between the rams and the goats.**

The Bible say's in Ezekiel 20:37 that God will cause you to pass under the Rod, and I will bring you into the bond of the covenant; 38 And I will purge out from among you the rebels, and them that transgress against me. I will bring them forth out of the country where they sojourn, and they shall not enter into the land of Israel: And Ye shall know that I am the Lord.

Passing under the rod of inspection and then he will purge out those that transgress against him.

Let the wheat and the tare grow together and God himself will do the separating at time of harvest; Matthew 13:24

Jeremiah 13:17 But if you will not listen, My soul will weep in secret for your pride, My eyes will weep bitterly and run down with tears, Because the Lords Flock has been taken Captive. Jeremiah 13:7

We Must listen so that we're not taken captive by Satan. We must study his devices within balance So we can see when he is on board hiding in plain sight, He has no new tricks just New Faces. And the Lord is also telling us here Through his Rod Of Inspection that everybody cannot go along With Us, Some will be purged Out In time to come, Don't be Surprised When the time Comes If it's the Person you started out with from the beginning ,Or Perhaps Your BFF/ Prayer Partner / Girlfriend/God Mother Of Children.. "Ohh Kapoowee" Get Over It! And I Mean Fast as you can, Because If you remain to long focusing on Lord Why? Like I did" you'll Loose ground and time worrying, We want to be gaining ground Not loosing, Pray for them and Move on "Know how much Jesus Loves you and has chosen you for such a time as this.

Having A Form Of Godliness But denying The Power thereof; from such turn away 2 Timothy 3:5 and the verse above says highminded lovers of pleasures more than lovers Of God, and A true Christian Will always be God Minded, If you got God you got power, to cast down, to overthrow to root out, And to pull down, Power to live right and talk right.. I'm saying this because many are in our mist riding off our prayers and our anointing and they are laying snares behind our backs, only God knows the heart, "you know?" When I meet someone new I ask the Lord" Lord God Show me their heart and he will do it!

I write this book to expose wickedness, darkness and to educate because I'm telling you as the day's get closer to Jesus' return the more we need to be aware of Satan's tricks. I know that they hated Jesus so of course I will be hated too we're not wanted on the jobs .."Listen Every Job I have ever had I mean ever had I always encountered Witchcraft someone trying to get rid of me, move me off the job and I'm pretty much use it, The Lord told me that I'm a big fish" Yes meaning that everyone wants to catch me, And the Devil will use anybody he can even the members of my own household; So anyway on this last position there were a few after me but God gave me strategy I walk right through their traps then one night I was talking to a coworker we work the night shift 10 to 6 am she and I was sitting at a table talking this woman and I got along very well she being in her mid50's Me 49 years young; I always enjoyed her no she wasn't saved but she would let me pray for her and ask for prayer. So' on this night there wasn't much to do at this time residents were asleep, the enemy comes a sit down at the table with us and we both know she dislikes me but she likes the other woman because they were working together before I got there, so we didint stop talking we glanced pleasantly in her direction, but kept talking even thoe she couldn't stand me, I was ok that she came over to sit with us,, looking back.. because once I saw her, standing by my food one evening we we're working together same shift; lets refer to her as 22' I would have to hide my lunch in odd places in the building like vacant rooms where other residents had previously passed away or family members had removed A loved one for just whatever reason but nevertheless all rooms had working refrigerators in them.

Or I'd have to leave it in the hot car for awhile while id go inside walk around first so that her 22, or her crew would not see me carrying a bag and then later go in search for my bag yes it was that bad. Id check at the top of the road where Id turn onto the job property, she would have stones and sticks in the driveway entrance and coins by my car, but she still couldn't stop me from coming, well that night she sat down and started to play with her phone she's 22 years old let me say how she held her phone in the air and took a pic of me." And on top of that she recorded my voice and took it to a root worker and paid them to cast a spell to remove me from the work place.

That was a new one on me, I thought for sure I' pretty much knew all or mostly all of the enemies tricks, that" was a new one on me! But I thank God because I needed to know That! to add It to this book, Aha'' There Is a time When Evil Serves Gods Purpose.

## POINTS Of CONTACT/ ACCURSED THINGS

Mr, Bern Zumpano Of Word Of Faith International – Miami FL

Say's that Removing the accursed thing is a form of deliverance and I do agree, Because after its removed from A House, Car, Office, Etc then that place shall receive freedom from oppression, I think about it kinda like a thirsty dry place that water cannot reach although the water is standing right outside the door just waiting for someone to open it; meanwhile the place is constantly drying up and the dry ground is beginning to crack and separate due to a lack of moisture, there is something holding their deliverance up or back in this case Scenario it's a door, That game show comes to mind What's behind door #1 Witches and Evil Workers know the trick Oh so well about points of contact, gifts and let me just say it does not have to be gift, it could be a stash from a visitor, they use this to gain entrance through the spiritual realm. It will be something that is very nice and appealing to the eye, Maybe even expensive whatever that would cause the targeted Individual to keep the accursed thing (gift) in his or her company as long as possible years even, they would hope.

Once You find out that you have an evil object NEVER give it away to someone else, because all that demon wants to do is find another address where it can set up and start up its Ministry again through that object whatever it's ministry might be meaning what it was design and created to do and be at its, evil birth remember Clothing, Shoes, A ,Vase, Jewelry, Anything, big or small it dosen't matter, an evil spirit can be attached to any object even a stick of gum.

**WATER SPIRTS.** This kind, this type, this class, Only comes out but by Prayer and fasting. .Mark 9:22 Check it out!

**Tree Magic The Worship of Trees.**

I Love to see full rich beautiful deep green in color trees of any kind, mostly along the road side while on a country road while driving through I'm from the south so I'm familiar with such sights or even in the back yard of a nice home; and the bigger they are the more shade One gives off On a Hot Summer lemonade Sweet Ice Tea day, that's what I think of when "I see or think, of A tree; Nothing about what I was about to learn.

I knew that trees carried a something spiritual Specialness about them and then there be some you'd see and wonder what happen to that tree?" all broken down dried out and thirsty looking no leaf's no life no breath no sway in the wind almost resembles a bare stick sticking up from the ground and then There those that you grew up with as a kid. Some carry that healthiness to them like the kind the Bible speaks of in

Psalms1:3 A tree planted by the rivers of water that bring forth his fruit in his season his leaf also shall not wither and what so ever he doeth shall prosper.

How could God's Trees be used to do and create evil to harm or hold someone to a certain place

Well" This is what I found Out"

Any portion of a sacred tree that's been chosen by a Witchdoctor or Witch for ritual purposes can be chopped and cut down and grinded into some type of powder to be placed and thrown around or inside their enemies homes cars businesses or work places or Get this" into the very food that they are eating and the Water their drinking.

They cut it's branches and fashioned them into magic wands to manipulate energy "So I read" But it went on to say that Witches would rather make his/her own wand than purchasing it because they believe when they make it themselves their own energy and their own power gets bonded with that tool.. they don't want it near any water; They may also own more than one, they may decorate it with tassels and glitter shiny and sparkley, type stuff and so forth. I didn't realize how much went into this wand I thought this would be something I'd simply minichen and quickly move on but it was too much to leave unsaid, I believe Theyve even taken time to clean the thing, so it diffinitely means something to them. To clean it they use Smoke or Selenite stone they lay it near for a few hours and or days this Stone they believe it shields a person or Space from outside influences this Stone is used in many kinds of dark spiritual work.. "Their Kind of spiritual work" I might add.

The Tip of it is Special to them.. I want to Just be absolutely clear that I I'm in no way in any agreement with this So If I may.. I'm just going to lay it down here.. Amen Ok"

So the tip is used to touched the object or Idem and while touching the idem at this same time they are using visuization that they are laying down a power by seeing emaginary Crystals before their wicked eyes they imanaige this and at this moment the curse has been applied.

They use one hand to push things through and the other to be a receiving hand they refer to this hand as their power hand which they also use for scanning things for energetic properties.

This wand is made out of wood, apple wood is mostly preferred but I'm pretty sure there's more than one way to skin a cat.

TREES Spirits

Marine Spirits they can inhibit trees and rocks and live inside them for years undetected and be buried or placed in Ones yard. And where Marine spirits are there will always be Snakes Near By.

This is what the bible is referring to when it speaks of groves exodus Exodus34:13 KJB Just one scripture of Many" concerning groves and wooden Images and Asherah Poles Made By Way Of Trees.

The kingdom of darkness works with colors, Black, White, Green, Blue Rainbow Apatch Indian Colors. Anything can be used as an Occultic Object I'm reminded Of someone using the bread ties twist off a loaf of bread these ties come in many colors and are easy use for evil workers, They are mostly used in the laying of snares

Luke 19:30 Says go into the village opposite you Where as you enter you will find a colt tide on which, no one has ever sat loose it and bring it here now what was it tide to?" a tree right?" yes it was, these evil doers Tie things to trees, Alters and Groves go together, And burry things under them, Isa 45:20 There are those that Pray to wood, So many destinies have been tide to trees just as this colt was tied down but glory be to the Lord Jesus Christ he is untying Colts right this very minute.

There are also Family Trees. We all have one A diagram showing the relationships between people In Several generations Of A Family: genealogical tree. All It would take is One person In the Family to open the door to Satan through Witchcraft, Occult pratices , and bring a curse on the entire bloodline As soon as their evil alter knows your name, Satan is greedy he not Only wants your house but your brothers house too, and his children and so on, The best thing you can do is not open that door ever! Satan cannot help you, Satan can only cause you more problems If he's Involved he only comes to kill steal and destroy and deceive that's all he knows how to do. He loves to fight against marriage's it the Only thing he cannot duplicate.

MORE ON WITCHES & WARLOCKS...Fasting to make their evil powers stronger just as we fast, so do they" Satan is a Copy Cat after the things Of God. Witches are big on places things under trees

I Want To go Deeper...ROOTWORKERS

These are the ones that are mostly going into the graveyards to do their works. It Is called Root Works Be cause it is a lot of work involved these people work day and night Or over a time period of sometimes 21 to 30 days Mixing certain ingredients letting it sit for 9 days undisturbed then going back after the nine day's are over to begin a $2^{nd}$ part and sometimes a 3 rd and $4^{th}$ and 5 th step maybe more.. going through crushing processes grinding things into to a fine powder to only sprinkle on their victim's porch or car door or food etc anything the person will touch aiming for their bloodstream

Or even a gift before they give to you, this is deeper then Witchcraft and rebellion This is a level Of evil that is beyond anything you or I can imagine They Cannot wait for nighttime so they can drive to their targeted victims address and lay down their roots and snares.. Ok I'm going to try and explain this stuff as best as I can and the things that Root workers do. They are referred to as Root workers because they deal with the earth and the burial of things such as trees leaf's these ones love to burry something in front of someone's home or church, they aim to bring an ending of some sort to things.

I was Born in NYC, But was definitely raised in the South and My Family and Friends of the Family would always joke about this kind of carrying on many people visited these types of people but would not ever dare to tell..." in the small towns Of the south this is big time secret by those who do such things.. Politicians also, I read that,"…. in sports the ball that is going to be used in the game is kept under lock and key because of this very sort of thing

. People search Out these people usually because they want to take something from someone... A job, Someone's Spouse, Family, their home, Or revenge, Or Fear, Jealousy, greed, You do not have to be done anything wrong to the other Person for them to Search Out one of these type persons to to try to cause havoc in one's life (Psalms 141:9) is One of many that says this.. So they go to the root worker and depending on what service they want the rootworker will tell the person to bring something belonging to the person they prefer something that has not been wash that still has the persons DNA on it Or something they've touched, a Picture of them, If the person can get fingernails Clippings, Hair, an Old peace of chewed gum out the trash can, a used sanitary napkin Yes" that What I said.. Ok You get the Picture.. The Rootworker Will take the item the may burial it at the grave of someone most likely that has some type of resemblance of what issue the client wants at their time of Deaf.. The Work may call for cutting someone Off so the go to crossroads, Or A railroad track, and don't let me forget a river or some type of running water, They tie things together, They Burn things, Not only colored candles For instance Black and Purple For Separation of a couple.. I believe this is why Jesus said What I join together let No man put Us Under, He knew that people would be doing things like this, To try and divide and separate They use evil oils to anoint things, Such as we would to make something Holy Unto the Lord. The enemy is a copy Cat.

**Effigy Dolls.**

Wax Dolls or Voodoo Dolls, As I type those words I heard the holy spirit say name "Ben, I at this time in my life, I do not know anyone name Ben.. "but maybe you do, Glory be to God... I'd say pray, and ask the Father to reveal Ben, Father show Me is there anything I need to Know Concerning Ben. I will let the holy Spirit have his way. "Hallelujah Glory Be To God!

OK, Moving right along.. So

An Effigy Doll is a sculpted imaged Representing the individual to be afflicted. Once you come to know the steps of the enemy, We can stop and block him and his agents step by step, Starting with this satanic baptism I'm aware that Satan is a Copy Cat after the things Of God, But As My Dear Old Grandmother would say this takes the Cake!"

I Very much know this is real because Bless the Lord he told me that an old friend whom I no longer see had one Of Me, Yes he did not say that it wouldn't be formed but It will not Prosper against Us, Thank You Father for letting Us Know what's going On around Us.

So AS I lay down their evil steps you make Prayer against each step.. Amen! He Must Yield at the ground that has been taken from him.

They place them on evil alters, stick pins into them, write words on them for instance. I command Charlie to Propose to Me, I command Charlie to Marry My Daughter, they will repeat this over and over, IN hopes to influence the persons thoughts to make them do what they want them to do, Or better yet Something like this: Miss Brown is getting tired of this Job, Really Tired (repeat) Really Tired..." (catch my grift) They Will write things like this also in repeat on paper, But in this case they are working with wax dolls and thay will write on the skull or the dead od the homemade figure.. Hold it over fire the ex-friend of mine I know this is one of the things she was doing because I could feel the flames on my back But glory be to God He never let them hurt Me. They make all types of destructive Pronouncements over the figure Image.. keys Pins Padlocks needles, are placed on the image again the person represented by the image will begin to feel the torment, Even rejection can be placed on an individual lord help the one who do such acts they will suffer much by way of Gods judgment when time comes. Adam was made in the image of God, That's where they draw this evil doing from, see they copy the bible but turn all things holy around for evil. They do a Satanic Ritual By Baptizing the doll in the name of the person their making the doll to be of, and if, They can, they will do all they can to get something of the persons with their DNA Attached that has not been washed is preferably preferred they take the garment to the evil worker with great joy, it makes their image of the person to be more potent with stronger effect, If a Person's DNA is there while there making this image copy It makes the doll more stronger in the persons image they called Tag Locks, their looking to attach a nail clipping, hair strand, Or cut up a worn sock by the individual to use for its cloth wrapping and in the wrapping they stick herbs inside and paper the size of a fortune cookie naming it, and if they don't have anything to work with the evil worker will use the person's full name and birth day, talking to the doll as they go, thread wrapping it as a finishing it off with a tie off speech for instance John Doe this is you, You will do whatever I say; they may even use love oils there's all types of oils to be used (Dixie Love Oil. So I went into their world to pull out this information, You, Child Of God take this this information down and build on it and make prayers, With this information you can stop the kingdom of darkness from overtaking your house and spoiling your goods( Mark 3:27

Here are items used to form a doll like such.. A Cloth, Clay, Mud, Sticks, Playdough, Bread, Wax Candle, Paper, String, Fruits &Vegetables, Wood, Plants/Herbs. Anything that can be formed into a shape they will use, Rebuke their Activation Process they will breath air into the doll themselves as part of the activation and use Holy Water" Yes I said Holy Water, and If the Maker should decide they don't want this person anymore they will deactivate the doll by taking it apart..

Breaking it down. They say deactivate speech first. One doll maker inform me that she will make a self-decoy doll if she feels that she's under attack the decoy of herself will take the hits for her,

Rebuke their herbs.. their Chamomile for peace, coffee grains is used to promote energy, rosemary for protection, this is referred to as controlled Work. And the Evil Work In The Grave Yards Are Dirt Work

FIXED GAZED

BE aware if you see someone staring at You with a locked piercing stare, and whispering quietly, This Person Is sending Out Evil Incantations Chants Against You. I experienced this at a Job I Once worked, Young African girl sitting on a stool eyes followed me constantly around the room I was watching her lips move but No sound coming out.. I smiled at her showing Myself Friendly But she didn't want to be Friends She didn't want Me there. I Prayed let the Words of her mouth be bound and caged and sent to the feet of Jesus one By One as they come through her lips.

I have held on to this book longer than I feel I should have and plus God has said to me to hurry it along. He has plains for this Book, So In Saying that I want to get everything Into it to help The Body Of Christ I have more to say than I have time, Now Satan can Not Beat Our GOD Or get anything over On him, for the Lord created he him, But This Book IS To Expose his Strategies.

and Secrets and weapons of war against Us the children of God. I know the writings in this book are weighty and maybe even far out to some but every thing I write here is true and is knowledge On satans dirty little kingdom, I wish not to even capitalize his name. He gets No glory in this book or his cohorts. Some Information Is from research and some the Holy Ghost revealed While in Warfare. I leave You With

This Dear Reader Whatever is ones highest and purest desire is his purpose of ruin and WE Will NOT BE Compromised

CPSIA information can be obtained
at www.ICGtesting.com
Printed in the USA
BVHW081736130123
656258BV00002B/453